Carol

New Daylight

KU-757-669

Edited by Naomi Starkey

January–April 2009

Suggestions for using *New Daylight*

Find a regular time and place, if possible, where you can read and pray undisturbed. Before you begin, take time to be still and perhaps use the BRF prayer. Then read the Bible passage slowly (try reading it aloud if you find it over-familiar), followed by the comment. You can also use *New Daylight* for group study and discussion, if you prefer.

The prayer or point for reflection can be a starting point for your own meditation and prayer. Many people like to keep a journal to record their thoughts about a Bible passage and items for prayer. In *New Daylight* we also note the Sundays and some special festivals from the Church calendar, to keep in step with the Christian year.

New Daylight and the Bible

New Daylight contributors use a range of Bible versions, and you will find a list of the versions used in each issue at the back of the notes on page 154. You are welcome to use your own preferred version alongside the passage printed in the notes, and this can be particularly helpful if the Bible text has been abridged.

New Daylight affirms that the whole of the Bible is God's revelation to us, and we should read, reflect on and learn from every part of both Old and New Testaments. Usually the printed comment presents a straight-forward 'thought for the day', but sometimes it may also raise questions rather than simply providing answers, as we wrestle with some of the more difficult passages of Scripture.

New Daylight *is also available in a deluxe edition (larger format). Check out your local Christian bookshop or contact the BRF office, who can also give more details about a cassette version for the visually impaired. For a Braille edition, contact St John's Guild, 8 St Raphael's Court, Avenue Road, St Albans, AL1 3EH.*

Writers in this issue

Veronica Zundel is an Oxford graduate, writer and journalist. She lives with her husband and son in North London, where they belong to the Mennonite Church.

Tony Horsfall is a freelance trainer and associate of EQUIP, a missions programme based at Bawtry Hall near Doncaster. He is an elder of his local church in West Yorkshire, and regularly travels abroad leading retreats and Quiet Days. He has written *Mentoring for Spiritual Growth* for BRF.

Gordon Giles is a vicar in Enfield, north-west London, previously based at St Paul's Cathedral, where his work involved musical and liturgical responsibilities. He was ordained in the Anglican Church in 1995.

Margaret Silf is an ecumenical Christian, committed to working across and beyond the denominational divides. She devotes herself mainly to writing and accompanying others on their spiritual journey.

David Robertson has ministered in a variety of parishes since his ordination in 1979 and is currently a vicar in Halifax. He has written *Marriage—Restoring Our Vision* and *Collaborative Ministry* for BRF.

Rachel Boulding is Deputy Editor of the *Church Times*. Previously, she was Senior Editor at SPCK Publishing and then Senior Liturgy Editor at Church House Publishing. She lives in Dorset with her husband and son—and, during school terms, more than 70 teenage boys.

Jennifer Oldroyd worked for many years at the Ashburnham Place conference centre in East Sussex. She was Managing Editor for a major Christian publisher, and in the last few years has had published two books of study material for small groups.

David Winter is retired from parish ministry. An honorary Canon of Christ Church, Oxford, he is well known as a writer and broadcaster. His most recent book for BRF is *Pilgrim's Way*.

Stephen Rand is a writer and speaker who in recent years has shared his time between Jubilee Debt Campaign, persecuted church charity Open Doors, and Mainstream, a Baptist church leaders' network.

Naomi Starkey is the Editor of *New Daylight*. She also edits *Quiet Spaces*, BRF's prayer and spirituality journal, as well as commissioning BRF's range of books for adults.

Further BRF reading for this issue

For more in-depth coverage of some of the passages in these
Bible reading notes, we recommend the following titles:

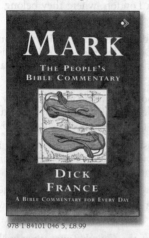

MARK

THE PEOPLE'S
BIBLE COMMENTARY

DICK
FRANCE
A BIBLE COMMENTARY FOR EVERY DAY

978 1 84101 046 5, £8.99

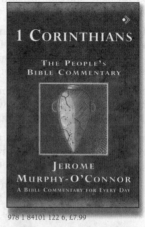

1 CORINTHIANS

THE PEOPLE'S
BIBLE COMMENTARY

JEROME
MURPHY-O'CONNOR
A BIBLE COMMENTARY FOR EVERY DAY

978 1 84101 122 6, £7.99

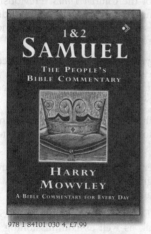

1 & 2 SAMUEL

THE PEOPLE'S
BIBLE COMMENTARY

HARRY
MOWVLEY
A BIBLE COMMENTARY FOR EVERY DAY

978 1 84101 030 4, £7.99

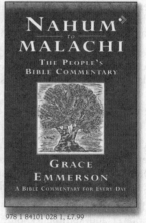

NAHUM to MALACHI

THE PEOPLE'S
BIBLE COMMENTARY

GRACE
EMMERSON
A BIBLE COMMENTARY FOR EVERY DAY

978 1 84101 028 1, £7.99

Naomi Starkey writes...

How do you feel about new years in general—and 2009 in particular? Do you enjoy starting a new calendar, wondering what will come to fill all those days and weeks? Or are you more inclined to think, 'Another year gone, and what have I managed to do?'

We may notice time rushing past when we receive a mailing from our old school, college or university and see how those who left years after us have risen more swiftly up the career ladder than us—or written that bestselling book or raised that lovely family. It can be a shock to realize that we are no longer 'the young people' and, in fact, even calling ourselves 'middle aged' is stretching a point.

With so much emphasis today on achieving goals and making the most of opportunities, it's easy to worry that we could have done more with our time. Alternatively, perhaps we feel that we must make some kind of change to our lives before it is too late, and (to paraphrase Alan Bennett's *A Private Function*) to make sure we 'have a future that lives up to our past'.

In this issue, we get to know a number of people (both in the Bible and from later centuries) who would probably be astonished that anybody remembered them in 2009. Far from achieving goals and meeting targets, they mostly had their lives violently cut short and none saw their God-given work come to maturity.

What we learn from Silas and Zechariah, from George, Mark, Alphege and Pierre Chanel, is that what really matters is obedience to our heavenly Father, whatever it costs. And in the events of Good Friday and Easter, we see the supreme example of this, as Jesus chose the way of the cross, something that he commands us to do likewise (Luke 9:23). As his followers, we must never forget that our lives are not our own but should be offered humbly to God to use for his purposes.

In this new year, God may be challenging us to renew our commitment to serve him. Instead of worrying about our own success (or lack of it), we need to listen out for his voice. He calls us to a pilgrim life, not a self-improvement programme, but he also promises that whatever the future has in store for us, he will be at our side (Matthew 28:20).

The BRF Prayer

Almighty God,
you have taught us that your word is a lamp for our feet
and a light for our path. Help us, and all who prayerfully
read your word, to deepen our fellowship with each other
through your love. And in so doing may we come to know you
more fully, love you more truly, and follow more faithfully in
the steps of your son Jesus Christ, who lives and reigns with
you and the Holy Spirit, one God for evermore. Amen.

Joining the faith

At the start of the year, it's good to think about spiritual beginnings and, in the next ten days, we are going to look at how we join the Christian faith, both inwardly and outwardly. Inevitably, that means we have to look at the often hotly disputed area of baptism. Bath or shower? Baby or believer? Two-stage or one? A book on baptism was called *The Water that Divides* (Donald Bridge and David Phypers, Christian Focus Publications, 1998) and, indeed, baptism is one of the central issues over which Christians disagree.

My own spiritual forebears were nicknamed 'Anabaptists' or 'rebaptizers' because, in the early stages of the movement, those who baptized believers were, in fact, rebaptizing people who had already been 'done' as infants, mostly in the Roman Catholic Church. So strongly did the Anabaptists believe in what they called 'believers' church' that they considered infant baptism a meaningless rite. Equally, however, I know Christian parents who feel strongly that children should be seen to be members of the household of faith from the start. Also, I know adults who value their baptism as an infant, re-affirmed in confirmation, as much as any Baptist values being baptized

as an adult. In the Bible, too, we read in Acts 16:33 of Paul and Silas' jailer that 'he and his entire family were baptized without delay'—so does that mean the babies were included?

We are all shaped in our belief by our own experience, of course. I am grateful that my humanist parents didn't have me 'christened' as a baby because it meant that I could choose myself to be baptized (by full immersion) at the age of 16. My parents attended and were clearly moved. My experience is that few things are more moving than a Baptist baptism ceremony, with silence as each candidate makes the promises, then a big splash followed by the congregation bursting out into a verse of a rousing hymn.

Sometimes I feel that our obsession with how someone begins as a Christian is a bit like asking every married couple 'How did you meet?' when, actually, the current state of their marriage is a lot more important than what their first date was like! So, I'll attempt in these notes to be fair to different traditions, remembering that, however we began, we are all travelling together in the journey of following Jesus.

Veronica Zundel

A painful beginning

God said to Abraham, 'As for you, you shall keep my covenant, you and your offspring after you throughout their generations. This is my covenant, which you shall keep, between me and you and your offspring after you: Every male among you shall be circumcised. You shall circumcise the flesh of your foreskins, and it shall be a sign of the covenant between me and you. Throughout your generations every male among you shall be circumcised when he is eight days old, including the slave born in your house and the one bought with your money from any foreigner who is not of your offspring.'

Most groups have some way of marking a new individual's entry. It may be as simple as filling in a registration form or as brutal as the 'initiation ceremonies' described in accounts of Victorian public school life, not to mention American college fraternities. The weight of ceremony given to a new member's entry often depends on how seriously membership is taken. My church, which sees membership as a substantial commitment, has a 'novice membership' scheme lasting at least six months, often more.

I knew a man who was circumcised for medical reasons. He couldn't walk properly for a week! This account of Abram being circumcised at 99 and his son Ishmael at 13 (vv. 24–25) is enough to make our eyes water. Circumcision at eight days, prescribed for future generations, is probably less traumatic, but still a significant action to perform on an infant. In the Jewish tradition, however, it is an occasion for both tears and rejoicing: tears because no parent feels good about surgery, however minor, on their baby and rejoicing because the boy is being welcomed into the community of faith.

Notice that this ceremony is exclusive to males; girls and women belonged to God's covenant people by association with a man, whether that was a father, husband or brother. We will return to this later. Meanwhile, we can note that, just as membership of a group brings both privileges and obligations, so beginning the faith involves both loss and gain. What we lose is worth losing, though, for the new life we gain.

Reflection

Today is the feast of the Naming and Circumcision of Jesus, which we will read about tomorrow. What does it mean to you that Jesus was a Jew?

VZ

Born to belong

After eight days had passed, it was time to circumcise the child; and he was called Jesus, the name given by the angel before he was conceived in the womb. When the time came for their purification according to the law of Moses, they brought him up to Jerusalem to present him to the Lord (as it is written in the law of the Lord, 'Every firstborn male shall be designated as holy to the Lord'), and they offered a sacrifice according to what is stated in the law of the Lord, 'a pair of turtledoves or two young pigeons'.

This short account actually has three distinct elements. First, the circumcision of Jesus at eight days old, which confirms that he belongs to the Jewish people. Second, the 'purification' of Mary 40 days after childbirth—a ritual that is foreign to us now as we no longer see childbearing as 'polluting'. Third, there is the sacrifice Mary and Joseph make to 'redeem' their firstborn, as every firstborn male belonged to God.

It is at his circumcision that Jesus receives the name God has given him through the angel Gabriel—a name meaning 'God saves'. It is much more than just a label as it points to his destiny. His identity is only revealed as he joins the community of God's people, which is telling: it is in relating to others, in belonging, that we truly find out who we are personally.

For better or worse, our Western society is becoming less and less 'officially Christian'. Still, many new parents look to the Church to provide a ceremony in which they can give thanks for their children, welcome them into the community and give them their names. How should the Church respond?

Traditions such as the Mennonites, who practise adult baptism, still tend to hold a thanksgiving or dedication service for a new baby (it is less well known that the Anglican Church can offer this, too). Such a service tells us that we are welcomed by God—as Jesus was—long before we can actually do anything for God or others ourselves. As the child's prayer says, God must like people a lot, because he makes so many of them.

Prayer

We bless you for our creation, preservation, and all the blessings of this life.

Anglican General Thanksgiving prayer

VZ

Washed and ready to serve

As it is written in the prophet Isaiah, 'See, I am sending my messenger ahead of you, who will prepare your way; the voice of one crying out in the wilderness: "Prepare the way of the Lord, make his paths straight"', John the baptizer appeared in the wilderness, proclaiming a baptism of repentance for the forgiveness of sins. And people from the whole Judean countryside and all the people of Jerusalem were going out to him, and were baptized by him in the river Jordan, confessing their sins.

At school, I once played Eliza Doolittle in Shaw's play *Pygmalion*. Arriving at Professor Henry Higgins' house for the first time, I declared, 'I washed my face and hands afore I come.' Washing before a big occasion is a normal human action. It is also part of many religious actions. Muslims, for instance, wash before entering the mosque and bathe before reading the Koran.

Ritual washing was a common practice in first-century Judaism and baptism was used to admit converts to the Jewish faith. The focus of John's baptism was on repentance of sins and he accompanied it with strongly worded moral directives (see Luke 3:10–14). The person who had been 'washed' was expected to endeavour to 'stay clean' afterwards.

Why was John sent ahead of Jesus to perform this ministry? Perhaps his father's prayer in Luke 1:77 gives a clue: 'to give knowledge of salvation to his people by the forgiveness of their sins'. Salvation can mean little to us unless we recognize that we need to be saved and John's uncompromising preaching certainly confronted people with their inadequacies. Baptism, then, was a way of physically expressing a desire to live differently.

Obsessive–compulsive disorder usually includes a compulsion to wash continually. This disorder shows us that feelings about dirt and cleansing are rooted deep in human psychology. That is why baptism is such a powerful symbolic act. Most Christian traditions call it a 'sacrament'—a word derived from the Latin for an oath. In the ceremony, we make a binding commitment, one that cannot be entered into lightly.

Prayer
'Wash me thoroughly from my iniquity, and cleanse me from my sin'
(Psalm 51:2).

VZ

Baptized into suffering?

Then Jesus came from Galilee to John at the Jordan, to be baptized by him. John would have prevented him, saying, 'I need to be baptized by you, and do you come to me?' But Jesus answered him, 'Let it be so now; for it is proper for us in this way to fulfil all righteousness.' Then he consented. And when Jesus had been baptized, just as he came up from the water, suddenly the heavens were opened to him and he saw the Spirit of God descending like a dove and alighting on him. And a voice from heaven said, 'This is my Son, the Beloved, with whom I am well pleased.' Then Jesus was led up by the Spirit into the wilderness to be tempted by the devil.

'The one who is more powerful than I is coming after me... I have baptized you with water; but he will baptize you with the Holy Spirit' (Mark 1:7–8). So says John the Baptist to those he is baptizing, but why does Jesus, whom John describes as the one who 'ranks ahead of me' (John 1:15), need to be baptized?

John himself asks that question and Jesus offers him only an enigmatic answer—'to fulfil all righteousness'. Some have seen Jesus' baptism as fully identifying with us, who are sinners. Others—and this is an ancient heresy—see his baptism as the moment when he 'becomes' the Son of God.

I believe that Jesus was the true image of God from his conception, so his baptism is not in any sense the beginning of his life of serving God. Nevertheless, it is the beginning of his public ministry. The Spirit descending like a dove (inspiring centuries of good and bad art!) and the voice from heaven declare what has always been true of Jesus, but which is only now revealed.

In some ways, the last verse of today's reading is the most significant. Jesus' baptism is not the prelude to a great display of God's power—instead, he is led into the desert, both literally and spiritually.

We, like him, are baptized not only into a new life, but into challenge, growth and, perhaps, suffering. It is not for nothing that, in early baptisms, candidates were held under water until they nearly drowned.

Reflection

Baptism is not a cheap ticket into heaven.

VZ

Catching the wind

Now there was a Pharisee named Nicodemus, a leader of the Jews. He came to Jesus by night and said to him, 'Rabbi, we know that you are a teacher who has come from God; for no one can do these signs that you do apart from the presence of God.' Jesus answered him, 'Very truly, I tell you, no one can see the kingdom of God without being born from above.' Nicodemus said to him, 'How can anyone be born after having grown old? Can one enter a second time into the mother's womb and be born?'

'Not a lot of people know' (as the comedian says) that the phrase 'born again' only appears in some translations of the Bible. An alternative translation, which appears here in the NRSV, is 'born from above'.

What does it mean to be 'born from above'? I don't think Nicodemus' questions arise out of too literal a view (he was, after all, a member of the Jewish council and not an ignorant man). Rather, I think there is a note of sarcasm in his response—he wasn't born yesterday, so to speak, and he knows that there is no such thing as starting your life over again. Or is there? 'For mortals,' Jesus might have added, 'it is impossible, but not for God; for God all things are possible' (Mark 10:27).

Christians have many theories about 'becoming a Christian'. Some of us expect people to have a standardized 'conversion experience' on a particular date that they can refer back to—a bit like being given a certificate. Others expect a slow process that is then expressed publicly in baptism or confirmation.

God does not seem to be limited by our ideas. The one thing we can say with certainty is that God will do the unexpected: 'The wind blows where it chooses, and you hear the sound of it, but you do not know where it comes from or where it goes. So it is with everyone who is born of the Spirit' (John 3:8). What is important is not when or how we came to follow Jesus, but that we do follow him.

Prayer

Holy Spirit, help me to be aware of your presence.

VZ

ACTS 2:36–38, 41 (NRSV)

How to be born

[Peter said] 'Therefore let the entire house of Israel know with certainty that God has made him both Lord and Messiah, this Jesus whom you crucified.' Now when they heard this, they were cut to the heart and said to Peter and to the other apostles, 'Brothers, what should we do?' Peter said to them, 'Repent, and be baptized every one of you in the name of Jesus Christ so that your sins may be forgiven; and you will receive the gift of the Holy Spirit...' So those who welcomed his message were baptized, and that day about three thousand persons were added.

Reading accounts of past revivals has made me aware that fashions in conversion appear to change through the centuries. There have been times when no one was seen as having truly been converted unless they spent hours or even days lamenting their sins, shedding copious tears and despairing of God ever accepting them.

It seems that Peter didn't require any such displays. True, his hearers are 'cut to the heart' by his account of Jesus, but he doesn't encourage them to remain at this point. It's notable, too, that the sermon which has had this effect on them is not all about what miserable sinners they are. It is all about who Jesus was and is.

Their decision to follow Jesus does, however, have different stages. First, they recognize who Jesus is. Second, they become aware of their own sinfulness. Third, they turn away from their old lives and are baptized into the new life of following Jesus. Fourth, they are promised the gift of the Holy Spirit—and notice that this is presented as an integral part of their conversion, not an added extra. There is a glorious variety of ways in which people come to Jesus, but if there is a 'normal Christian birth', these elements must surely belong in it, whether the 'labour' is short or long.

Finally, we are told, 'they devoted themselves to the apostles' teaching and fellowship, to the breaking of bread and the prayers' (v. 42) and that they treated all their goods as common and gave to those in need. Unless a life of positive discipleship follows on baptism, the baptism is meaningless.

Reflection

Acts tell us the new believers had 'the goodwill of all the people' (v. 47). Do we? Should we?

VZ

Taking the plunge

The eunuch asked Philip, 'About whom, may I ask you, does the prophet say this, about himself or about someone else?' Then Philip began to speak, and starting with this scripture, he proclaimed to him the good news about Jesus. As they were going along the road, they came to some water; and the eunuch said, 'Look, here is water! What is to prevent me from being baptized?' He commanded the chariot to stop, and both of them, Philip and the eunuch, went down into the water, and Philip baptized him.

When my son was a baby, we got to know a neighbour who was in the process of very slowly becoming a Christian. Her faith grew as she talked to us and to her daughter, who was already a believer. However, she was very reluctant to be baptized as members of her family, who were Jehovah's Witnesses, taught that, if you sin after you are baptized, you cannot be forgiven.

This is an ancient belief that led early Christians to delay baptism until their deathbed, so that they had no chance to sin after it. Though it's possible to use scripture to support such a belief, it's also quite easy to find writings that refute it, such as 1 John 1:8–10.

The New Testament pattern is quite different: baptism follows as hot on the heels of repentance and belief as is humanly possible. The Ethiopian eunuch's words to Philip—'Look, here is water'—may be part of an ancient baptism liturgy. Perhaps his words 'What is to prevent me?' are an equivalent of the 'If anyone knows just cause' words in a wedding service, giving an opportunity for anyone to raise valid objections to the ceremony.

There are, of course, other reasons for someone delaying baptism—for instance, if they were baptized as an infant but wish to affirm their faith as an adult and are not sure about being 'rebaptized'. Generally speaking, baptism belongs at the beginning of our journey of faith. It is a visible, tangible sign of the new life we are beginning. We may disagree about who should be baptized and when, but I hope we can agree that Christian life should begin with a splash!

Reflection
Do you turn to Christ?
I turn to Christ.

From the Anglican baptism rite

VZ

A welcoming gift

While Apollos was in Corinth, Paul passed through the interior regions and came to Ephesus, where he found some disciples. He said to them, 'Did you receive the Holy Spirit when you became believers?' They replied, 'No, we have not even heard that there is a Holy Spirit.' Then he said, 'Into what then were you baptized?' They answered, 'Into John's baptism.' Paul said, 'John baptized with the baptism of repentance, telling the people to believe in the one who was to come after him, that is, in Jesus.' On hearing this, they were baptized in the name of the Lord Jesus. When Paul had laid his hands on them, the Holy Spirit came upon them, and they spoke in tongues and prophesied.

Here's another divisive issue. Many Christians have used this passage to argue for a two-stage conversion: first we are baptized with water, then later with the Holy Spirit. Jesus' words to Nicodemus about being born 'of water and Spirit' (John 3:5) have also been used this way.

It's true I personally experienced something that could be called 'baptism in the Spirit' a few years after becoming a Christian, but it was in the context of making a deeper commitment to God. Despite such experiences, I don't think there's any good reason to put a permanent wedge between water baptism and 'Spirit baptism'. The believers we read of in Ephesus are in a unique position as followers of John the Baptist. They have only learnt about baptism as being for repentance. They can't have listened very carefully to John, who promised that Jesus would baptize them with the Holy Spirit (Mark 1:8).

The situation is different for us: we are baptized in the name of Father, Son and Spirit. Receiving the Holy Spirit is part and parcel of becoming a Christian—we do not just assent to a set of teachings; we are filled with new life. As I came up out of the water of baptism nearly 40 years ago, I had a strong conviction that this was when my new life began.

When we come to Jesus we repent, believe, are baptized *and receive the Spirit*. No story is complete without its end. We can, of course, be 'refilled' with the Spirit any time we ask.

Prayer

Lord, fill me with your Spirit.

VZ

Into death—and out

What then are we to say? Should we continue in sin in order that grace may abound? By no means! How can we who died to sin go on living in it? Do you not know that all of us who have been baptized into Christ Jesus were baptized into his death? Therefore we have been buried with him by baptism into death, so that, just as Christ was raised from the dead by the glory of the Father, so we too might walk in newness of life. For if we have been united with him in a death like his, we will certainly be united with him in a resurrection like his… For whoever has died is freed from sin. But if we have died with Christ, we believe that we will also live with him.

When I was a teenager with troubles at home, I wished I could sleep for a week and then begin my life again, make a completely fresh start. It took me many years to realize that's just what I did in my baptism: I 'died to sin' so that I might be 'alive to God' (Romans 6:11). That is one reason for my being so attached to total immersion: no other form of baptism so completely expresses that idea of death and rising from death for me.

'I have a baptism with which to be baptized, and what stress I am under until it is completed!' (Luke 12:50). So said Jesus to his disciples, using baptism as a symbol of the death to which he was heading. Baptism is more than a feel-good occasion when we celebrate our faith. Like circumcision, it is a serious action as well as a joyful one. We are baptized into a life with Jesus, but that also means a demanding life, a life with the potential for suffering, for 'the Lord disciplines those whom he loves' (Hebrews 12:6, quoting Proverbs 3:12).

The commitment we make in baptism is a commitment to living the Jesus way, which means resisting wrong in ourselves and in the world. In other words, it means battles, though our weapons are not physical ones (Ephesians 6:12). The end product, however, is not death but life.

Reflection

'You have already been cleansed by the word that I have spoken to you' (John 15:3).

VZ

All together now

In Christ Jesus you are all children of God through faith. As many of you as were baptized into Christ have clothed yourselves with Christ. There is no longer Jew or Greek, there is no longer slave or free, there is no longer male and female; for all of you are one in Christ Jesus. And if you belong to Christ, then you are Abraham's offspring, heirs according to the promise.

Remember at the beginning of these notes I remarked that circumcision was a sign of belonging that was only applied to male babies? Today's reading is the point at which all that changed.

Baptism is a sign for *all* believers—it is not limited to boys and men. In Christ, therefore, there is no distinction between male and female. A baptized woman belongs to Christ not through her husband's or father's or brother's baptism, but through her own. That is certainly good news for women.

Not only does this take away the distinction between male and female in Christ, but between Jew and Greek, slave and free. In each of these pairs, one of the pair was traditionally circumcised, the other not (Greeks were uncircumcised and most slaves would be Gentiles). From this point on all are one body in Christ—called by the same Lord, initiated with the same sign, sealed with the same Spirit (see 2 Corinthians 1:22). Assimilated first-century Jewish

men who wanted to enter the Greek athletics, where athletes competed naked, often had cosmetic surgery to attempt to hide the fact that they were circumcised. Baptism does not show in a physical way (at least once we've dried off!), but its effects should be visible in our lives. It makes each one of us heirs to God's promises and children of an all-loving Father: 'And because you are children, God has sent the Spirit of his Son into our hearts, crying, "Abba! Father!"' (Galatians 4:6). Why would we want to hide that?

Reflection

'Abba, Father.' What does it mean to you today to be a child of God? If your own experience of a father is mixed or absent, can your relationship with God bring healing in this area? Pray for God to show you what difference it makes to be God's beloved child.

VZ

2 Samuel 1—7

The story of David in the Old Testament is a gripping one, packed with excitement and adventure, heroism and romance, triumph and tragedy. He appears to be a man of great passion and intensity, a warrior with a poet's heart—tough yet tender, strong yet vulnerable.

From his youth, David lived with the knowledge of God's calling for him to give his life to leading the people of Israel. The biblical narratives reveal to us the unfolding of God's plan for both him and the nation. We are privileged to be able to watch how the Lord shapes his servant through the ups and downs of his life, taking him from shepherd boy to ruler of all Israel.

The section we are reading together here covers the transition between the death of Saul and David's establishment as king in Jerusalem—a time of turmoil and tension. Despite all the uncertainty, we can recognize the guiding hand of God bringing his purposes to pass.

We meet David in his early 20s and follow his life for the next seven and a half years as he returns from enforced exile among the Philistines and settles again in Hebron (2 Samuel 5:4–5). It is not clear if David returned with an idea in his mind of how things would work out, but we can identify a definite progression in the events that take place—a respectful marking of the end of Saul's reign, the reuniting of the people of Israel after a period of civil war, recognition of David's right to be king, the strategic choice of Jerusalem as capital, defeat of the Philistines and restoration of worship with the return of the ark of the covenant. The section closes with a revelation from God about his future plans for the house of David and a heartfelt prayer of thanksgiving from the newly established king.

David was chosen because he was a man after God's own heart (1 Samuel 13:14), but he was far from perfect. Indeed, his own testimony was this: 'And today, though I am the anointed king, I am weak' (2 Samuel 3:39). It is those words that endear David to us. Yes, he was a man of great spiritual insight and passion, but he was also human and flawed like the rest of us. If we look carefully, we will see ourselves reflected in his story and those of his contemporaries.

Tony Horsfall

2 SAMUEL 1:2, 4, 11–14 (NIV)

David hears of Saul's death

On the third day a man arrived from Saul's camp, with his clothes torn and with dust on his head. When he came to David, he fell to the ground to pay him honour… He said, 'The men fled from the battle. Many of them fell and died. And Saul and his son Jonathan are dead.' … Then David and all those with him took hold of their clothes and tore them. They mourned and wept and fasted till evening for Saul and his son Jonathan, and for the army of the Lord and the house of Israel, because they had fallen by the sword. David said to the young man who brought him the report, 'Where are you from?' 'I am the son of an alien, an Amalekite,' he answered. David asked him, 'Why were you not afraid to lift your hand to destroy the Lord's anointed?'

For several years, David had been on the run from Saul, who wanted to kill him. His irrational jealousy made David's life a misery. Saul stood in the way of his becoming king and his fractured personality had caused the disintegration of the nation. Surely David would be glad to see him gone? That is what the Amalekite reasoned as he brought news of Saul's demise. Far from rejoicing at his rival's tragic end, however, David is heart-broken.

Twice David had the opportunity to kill Saul himself, but refused to do so because he recognized that Saul was still the Lord's anointed (1 Samuel 24:5–7; 26:9–11). David was prepared to wait for God to establish him as king rather than force matters by acting presumptuously. Such patience is not always found in young leaders with ambition and calling.

David's grief is genuine. He mourns for Saul because, in better days, the king had been good to him, and Saul's son, Jonathan, had been his closest friend. He mourns for the army of Israel, defeated and humiliated by the Philistines. He mourns for the whole nation, broken, dispirited and leaderless. It is not a moment for the cold calculation of personal ambition or political opportunism. It is a time to weep with those who weep and feel as the heart of God feels for a nation in turmoil.

Prayer

*Lord, help me to feel the pain
of others.*

TH

2 Samuel 1:17–27 (NIV, abridged)

David's lament for Saul and Jonathan

David took up this lament concerning Saul and his son Jonathan, and ordered that the people of Judah be taught this lament of the bow (it is written in the Book of Jashar): 'Your glory, O Israel, lies slain on your heights. How the mighty have fallen! … Saul and Jonathan—in life they were loved and gracious, and in death they were not parted. They were swifter than eagles, they were stronger than lions… I grieve for you, Jonathan my brother; you were very dear to me. Your love for me was wonderful, more wonderful than that of women. How the mighty have fallen!'

A lament is a passionate expression of grief, a heartfelt cry of sadness. Here David, who composed some of the most memorable and uplifting songs of praise, allows himself the opportunity to pour out his heart to God because of his deep sorrow.

Christians are sometimes confused about how to express their grief. Some contemporary teaching has emphasized the power of praise and praising God in all circumstances, so they feel guilty about the pain inside them and do not know how to release it. While Paul does say we are not to 'grieve like the rest' (1 Thessalonians 4:13), he means that we should not grieve in the hysterical way that may characterize those with no hope in God. He does not mean that we should not grieve at all or suppress our true feelings. That would be cruel, unnatural and unhealthy. Grief is best acknowledged and expressed, in a way that is consistent with our belief in heaven.

David's own heart feels the loss of his dearest friend, Jonathan, most keenly. Those who have known the loss of a soulmate will understand the depth of his feeling and the pain in his heart. His lament enables him to get in touch with his grief, express it and so begin the slow process of healing and recovery.

If you are grieving today, may I encourage you to pour your heart out to God. You could pray aloud or write your prayer down. You may find a song that helps or a piece of music. You might talk with a trusted friend. You may just want a good cry. Remember, it's OK to grieve.

Prayer

Lord, comfort all who mourn today.

TH

2 Samuel 2:1–4 (NIV)

David anointed king of Judah

In the course of time, David enquired of the Lord. 'Shall I go up to one of the towns of Judah?' he asked. The Lord said, 'Go up.' David asked, 'Where shall I go?' 'To Hebron,' the Lord answered. So David went up there with his two wives, Ahinoam of Jezreel and Abigail, the widow of Nabal of Carmel. David also took the men who were with him, each with his family, and they settled in Hebron and its towns. Then the men of Judah came to Hebron and there they anointed David king over the house of Judah.

David's first move after Saul's death is to seek direction from God. Rather than jumping straight into action, he pauses to stop, think and ask God to guide him. Such dependency on God for wisdom and the ability to curb one's natural impulsiveness is a mark of spiritual maturity.

Hebron was a city of refuge, a place of safety (Joshua 21:13). Perhaps after his harrowing time on the run from Saul and following his exile among the Philistines, David needed to find a place to recover where he knew he would be welcomed and accepted.

More importantly, Hebron was an ancient place of worship, with deep spiritual significance in the history of Israel. It was where Abraham, Isaac and Jacob had been based and, therefore, strongly associated with the covenant promises that God had made to the patriarchs about the land that he would give them (see Genesis

13:18 and 35:27). Whether David realized it or not, we see here the intention of God to move forward in his gracious plans for Israel and continue the outworking of his promise to make it a great nation. It's as if God is saying, 'Let's go back to where we were and carry on from where we left off.'

For David, it must have been a most satisfying moment. At last the calling he had for his life, which he had held in secret for so long and for which he had had to wait so patiently, is being recognized by others. He is anointed as king, albeit only of the tribe of Judah. It will be seven long years before all Israel will recognize him, but at least he now knows that God is at work.

Prayer

*Lord, help me to trust in
your timing.*

TH

War between two houses

Meanwhile, Abner son of Ner, the commander of Saul's army, had taken Ish-Bosheth son of Saul and brought him over to Mahanaim. He made him king over Gilead, Ashuri and Jezreel, and also over Ephraim, Benjamin and all Israel. Ish-Bosheth son of Saul was forty years old when he became king over Israel, and he reigned two years. The house of Judah, however, followed David. The length of time David was king in Hebron over the house of Judah was seven years and six months.

The political vacuum created by Saul's death is now exploited by the commander of his army, who seems to be the equivalent of Mr Worldly Wise in Bunyan's *Pilgrim's Progress*. A strong, natural leader, he lives his life by using human wisdom and political cunning and his hunger for power is about to plunge the country into civil war.

Rather than taking time to think, as David had done, and enquire of the Lord, Abner rushes straight ahead with his ill-conceived plan to keep hold of power. There was never any suggestion in the fledgling Israelite monarchy that the king would be succeeded by his son, but Abner assumes that this should be the case—presumably because he can then become the power behind the throne. The expression 'he made him king' illustrates just how much this was a human appointment rather than a divine one and betrays the arrogance of the man.

Ambition is not in itself wrong, but, when it is driven by personal advantage, it becomes selfish ambition—one of the most destructive of all human motivations. It is the cause of much disunity and disharmony in churches and other organizations and we are warned against it by James in his letter: 'But if you harbour bitter envy and selfish ambition in your hearts, do not boast about it or deny the truth. Such "wisdom" does not come down from heaven but is earthly, unspiritual, of the devil. For where you have envy and selfish ambition, there you find disorder and every evil practice' (James 3:14–16).

Led astray by his own selfish ambition, Abner is about to lead his followers down a path of destruction that will ruin many lives and hold back the purposes of God.

Prayer

Save us, Lord, from our own foolish ways.

TH

David the peacemaker

The war between the house of Saul and the house of David lasted a long time. David grew stronger and stronger, while the house of Saul grew weaker and weaker... Then Abner sent messengers on his behalf to say to David, 'Whose land is it? Make an agreement with me, and I will help you bring all Israel over to you.' ... When Abner, who had twenty men with him, came to David at Hebron, David prepared a feast for him and his men. Then Abner said to David, 'Let me go at once and assemble all Israel for my lord the king, so that they may make a compact with you, and that you may rule over all that your heart desires.' So David sent Abner away, and he went in peace.

Once selfish ambition takes hold in a group of people, it gives birth to another highly destructive force—that of a biased spirit. This puts loyalty to a person or group beyond common sense and the doing of what is right and creates a 'win at all costs' mentality. Paul discovered its devastating effects at Corinth (1 Corinthians 1:10–13) and it has infected many churches since. In some parts of the world it can manifest itself in tribal disputes, in others in denominational rivalries.

David himself seems to have stood back from the conflict, although his supporters seem to have been equally at fault. We are not sure if Abner's approach to David is motivated by expediency, because his side is losing the war, or by recognition of the fact that David really has been appointed by God (see 2 Samuel 3:9–10, 18).

The old pride still seems to be there (as he boasts, 'If I do not do for David what the Lord promised him', v. 9) and we may suspect him of trying to strengthen his own position yet again (v. 6).

David, however, welcomes his approach with a gesture of forgiveness and reconciliation. A wise person once said that evil continues to multiply unless someone is willing to absorb the cost of it and bring it to an end. It would have been easy for David to look for revenge and seek out retributive justice, but, if the bloodshed and feuding is to end, someone must draw the line and David has the courage to do just that.

Prayer
Make me a channel of your peace, Lord.

TH

Joab murders Abner

When Joab and all the soldiers with him arrived, he was told that Abner son of Ner had come to the king and that the king had sent him away and that he had gone in peace. So Joab went to the king and said, 'What have you done? Look, Abner came to you. Why did you let him go? Now he is gone! You know Abner son of Ner; he came to deceive you and observe your movements and find out everything you are doing.' Joab then left David and sent messengers after Abner, and they brought him back from the well of Sirah. But David did not know it. Now when Abner returned to Hebron, Joab took him aside into the gateway, as though to speak with him privately. And there, to avenge the blood of his brother Asahel, Joab stabbed him in the stomach, and he died.

Our attention now focuses on Joab, a senior leader in David's army, whose brother Asahel has been killed by Abner. He represents the other side in the feud that has overtaken the nation and he is just as responsible for stoking up the fires of conflict as was Abner.

Joab seems to have been motivated by bitterness and the desire for revenge. What powerful forces these are within the human heart! His resentment towards Abner and the burning desire to settle an old score blind Joab to the bigger picture of the needs of the nation as a whole and the interests of the king he serve. Nor can he appreciate that Asahel's reckless pursuit of Abner contributed to his own death. Reason has been overruled by inflamed passion. He is unwilling to forgive.

Human 'anger does not bring about the righteous life that God desires' (James 1:20). Joab's treachery in deceiving and then murdering his rival must have stained his own soul and it brings down David's wrath on him, too. The author of the letter to the Hebrews warns us not to allow a 'bitter root' to grow in us because it will cause trouble (12:15). We do well to heed his guidance.

David seems not to have been involved in the murder and his personal integrity gives the general population confidence that they can trust him.

Prayer

Forgive our sins, Lord, as we forgive the sins of others.

TH

Ish-Bosheth is murdered

When Ish-Bosheth son of Saul heard that Abner had died in Hebron, he lost courage, and all Israel became alarmed... Now Recab and Baanah, the sons of Rimmon the Beerothite, set out for the house of Ish-Bosheth, and they arrived there in the heat of the day while he was taking his noonday rest. They went into the inner part of the house as if to get some wheat, and they stabbed him in the stomach... After they stabbed and killed him, they cut off his head. Taking it with them, they travelled all night by way of the Arabah. They brought the head of Ish-Bosheth to David at Hebron and said to the king, 'Here is the head of Ish-Bosheth son of Saul, your enemy, who tried to take your life. This day the Lord has avenged my lord the king against Saul and his offspring.'

The selfish ambition of Abner, the bitter envy of Joab and the rivalry between Israel and Judah have created the context for the shameful murder of an innocent man. Ish-Bosheth was no real threat to David, but, with the kind of opportunism typical of Abner, the two mercenaries seek to ingratiate themselves with the king.

We may be appalled by the violence we see here and feel morally superior to those whose lives are described for us, but we do well to remember that Jesus said harbouring hate-filled, vengeful thoughts is just as sinful as the actual act of murder (Matthew 5:21–22).

I have highlighted the sins of selfish ambition, envy and party spirit because I have seen how common they are among Christian people and what damage they cause within Christian organizations. Even when people have the highest motives and are involved in the noblest of causes, they can succumb to these powerful forces and unwittingly give evil a foothold. I have often counselled broken people who have been the victims of power plays, ungodly factions and aggressive, unspiritual individuals.

Once again, David rises above such carnal behaviour and roundly condemns the murderers. He seeks no advancement by wicked means. If his cause is to progress, it will be because God opens the way for him, not because he has brought it about by force.

Prayer

Cleanse my heart, O God. Renew a right spirit within me.

TH

2 SAMUEL 5:1–5 (NIV)

David becomes king over Israel

All the tribes of Israel came to David at Hebron and said, 'We are your own flesh and blood. In the past, while Saul was king over us, you were the one who led Israel on their military campaigns. And the Lord said to you, "You shall shepherd my people Israel, and you shall become their ruler."' When all the elders of Israel had come to King David at Hebron, the king made a compact with them at Hebron before the Lord, and they anointed David king over Israel. David was thirty years old when he became king, and he reigned for forty years. In Hebron he reigned over Judah for seven years and six months, and in Jerusalem he reigned over all Israel and Judah for thirty-three years.

For the third time, David is anointed as king and at last he is able to rule over a united Israel. His reign initiated one of the golden periods in Israel's history and, for the next 33 years, a man after God's own heart was on the throne.

Notice the three reasons given by the tribes of Israel for their support of David. First, his shared humanity. He was an Israelite like them, made of flesh and blood. He was godly but real, and people found him approachable and accessible. Second, his natural ability. He was the one who had been behind their major victories and they were secure in his leadership. Third, his divine authority. They knew what God had said to him even as a boy and their anointing of him was simply a confirmation of a divine appointment that

had already been made.

It is important to note the leadership metaphor used by God to describe David's role as king—'you will *shepherd* my people.' David was familiar with this image, of course, but it stands in contrast to many secular models of leadership, both then and now. It suggests a ruler who will care for his people, guide them in the right way, provide for them and protect them. At a time when his nation was broken and fragmented, his first job would be to draw the scattered flock together—a task that David was uniquely fit to carry out and for which God had slowly been preparing him.

Prayer

Guide all in leadership today,
Father.

TH

David conquers Jerusalem

The king and his men marched to Jerusalem to attack the Jebusites, who lived there. The Jebusites said to David, 'You will not get in here; even the blind and the lame can ward you off.'… Nevertheless, David captured the fortress of Zion… David then took up residence in the fortress and called it the City of David… And he became more and more powerful, because the Lord God Almighty was with him. Now Hiram king of Tyre sent messengers to David, along with cedar logs and carpenters and stonemasons, and they built a palace for David. And David knew that the Lord had established him as king over Israel and had exalted his kingdom for the sake of his people Israel.

The Jebusite stronghold of Zion had long been a thorn in the side of God's people after they entered the promised land. In capturing this particular fortress, David is not only ridding Israel of a potential threat to stability but also establishing a secure base from which to build his kingdom. In addition, he is laying the foundations of the most spiritually significant city in the world.

David's confidence that God is with him is bolstered by his capturing the hitherto impregnable city and he now moves home from Hebron to the fortress, which he renames the city of David. The name 'Zion' continues to be significant, however, and is used in scripture to describe the place where God makes his dwelling, as well as being a special name for his people. The practical help of a neighbouring king—Hiram of Tyre—in the building of a royal palace is also taken by David as an indication of God's blessing.

David 'became more and more powerful' (v. 10) or, in the words of THE MESSAGE, 'he proceeded with a longer stride, a larger embrace'. Peterson's intriguing paraphrase suggests that David moved forward boldly and confidently into the vision that God was giving him for the kingdom (the 'longer stride'), but at the same time he kept his heart open to the people around him and his call to be their shepherd (the 'larger embrace').

Christian leadership always seeks to balance a radical pursuit of God's vision with loving respect for his people.

Prayer

Give to your Church, Lord, wise and godly leaders.

TH

David defeats the Philistines

When the Philistines heard that David had been anointed king over Israel, they went up in full force to search for him, but David heard about it and went down to the stronghold. Now the Philistines had come and spread out in the Valley of Rephaim; so David enquired of the Lord, 'Shall I go and attack the Philistines? Will you hand them over to me?' The Lord answered him, 'Go, for I will surely hand the Philistines over to you.' So David went to Baal Perazim, and there he defeated them. He said, 'As waters break out, the Lord has broken out against my enemies before me.' So that place was called Baal Perazim. The Philistines abandoned their idols there, and David and his men carried them off.

It was inevitable that David would have to deal with Israel's long-term enemies, the Philistines. He didn't have to wait long, either—they came to seek out the newly anointed king, confident that they would do to him what they had done to Saul.

David may be growing in confidence, but it is a confidence rooted in God and he retains his sense of prayerful dependency. Instead of moving into action, he retires to the safety of his fortress to listen to God. Only when he has confirmation from God that he should indeed engage the enemy does he go forward into battle.

The ensuing battle is a major victory for Israel and a crushing defeat for the Philistines and their false gods. David describes it like gushing waters bursting forth and sweeping away the enemy and so the place is appropriately named 'Baal Perazim', which means 'the Lord who breaks out'. This is one of those occasions where God reveals something of himself through his actions and, from this point onwards, God is known as 'Lord of the breakthrough'. It is a name that has continued to encourage God's people to believe he can overwhelm their spiritual enemies and give victory to them in the most trying of circumstances.

A second battle follows (vv. 22–25); David's approach is exactly the same, although God gives him a very different strategy for defeating the enemy. The principle is clear: always take time to listen carefully to God before embarking on any major course of action.

Prayer

Guide my steps this day, Lord.

TH

28

The ark is brought to Jerusalem (1)

David again brought together out of Israel chosen men, thirty thousand in all. He and all his men set out from Baalah of Judah to bring up from there the ark of God, which is called by the Name, the name of the Lord Almighty, who is enthroned between the cherubim that are on the ark. They set the ark of God on a new cart and brought it from the house of Abinadab, which was on the hill... When they came to the threshing floor of Nacon, Uzzah reached out and took hold of the ark of God, because the oxen stumbled. The Lord's anger burned against Uzzah because of his irreverent act; therefore God struck him down and he died there beside the ark of God... David was afraid of the Lord that day and said, 'How can the ark of the Lord ever come to me?'

The next item on David's agenda is to transfer the ark of the covenant to Jerusalem, placing the worship of God at the centre of the nation's life. For years it had lain neglected in Kiriath-jearim—a metaphor for Israel's neglect of the Lord. That must now be put right if they are to be truly God's people.

There is no doubt that David's motives are pure and his thinking correct, but he has made two fatal mistakes. First, he has not consulted God as to the proper way to do this and, second, he has forgotten that there is a 'prescribed way' of transporting the ark—on two poles and carried by the priests (see 1 Chronicles 15:12–13).

One of the key lessons here is that God's work must be done in God's way. The ark should never have been carried on a cart or pulled by oxen, nor escorted by anyone other than the priests. The strange incident with Uzzah reveals a powerful spiritual lesson: we must never become overly familiar with the things of God or handle sacred things irreverently.

It was a sobering lesson for the new king and it affected him deeply. 'The fear of the Lord is the beginning of wisdom' (Proverbs 9:10) and, right at the start of his reign, a holy respect for sacred things is burned into his soul. It will be an important safeguard for the future.

Prayer

Save us, dear Lord, from the sin of presumption.

TH

The ark is brought to Jerusalem (2)

Now King David was told, 'The Lord has blessed the household of Obed-Edom and everything he has, because of the ark of God.' So David went down and brought up the ark of God from the house of Obed-Edom to the City of David with rejoicing... David, wearing a linen ephod, danced before the Lord with all his might... When David returned home to bless his household, Michal daughter of Saul came out to meet him and said, 'How the king of Israel has distinguished himself today, disrobing in the sight of the slave girls of his servants as any vulgar fellow would!' David said to Michal, '... I will celebrate before the Lord. I will become even more undignified than this, and I will be humiliated in my own eyes.'

Having had time to ponder the incident with Uzzah and hearing of the blessing on Obed-Edom as he shelters the ark (see v. 11), David now goes ahead with his plan, but this time much more carefully. The priests are involved, sacrifices are made and there is great rejoicing. It is a foretaste of the vibrant worship that characterizes David's reign.

It is interesting to note that the solemnity of yesterday's passage gives way to the unrestrained joyfulness described in today's reading. Reverence and rapture are not incompatible, but must be held in a creative tension. Reverence alone leads to a dead formalism; rapture by itself may become an empty frenzy.

David himself leads the worship with characteristic enthusiasm and a childlike forgetfulness regarding his royal status. It perhaps represents a release of pent-up emotion after years of being under pressure, but it is also a reminder to us of the deep and passionate faith that was moving within him and his spiritual anointing. We should not be afraid of his example.

Michal, his wife, as a jaundiced spectator, finds in his 'undignified' display a reason for contempt. At one time she loved him, but, since the death of her father, her love for him has grown cold and her inward bitterness is manifested in this vitriolic attack. It does nothing to dampen David's spirit, however, for he knows it is right to worship God with all his heart and soul and strength.

Prayer

Cause my soul to rejoice in you,
O Lord.

TH

God's promise to David

[Nathan the prophet said] 'The Lord declares to you that the Lord himself will establish a house for you: When your days are over and you rest with your ancestors, I will raise up your offspring to succeed you, who will come from your own body, and I will establish his kingdom. He is the one who will build a house for my Name, and I will establish the throne of his kingdom for ever. I will be his father, and he shall be my son. When he does wrong, I will punish him with a rod wielded by human beings, with floggings inflicted by human hands. But my love will never be taken away from him, as I took it away from Saul, whom I removed from before you. Your house and your kingdom shall endure for ever before me; your throne shall be established for ever.'

David wisely uses Nathan as a spiritual adviser and shares with him his desire to build a house for the ark—a thought with which the prophet concurs (vv. 1–3). However, God speaks to Nathan during the night to reject the idea (v. 4), saying that, instead, he will build a house for David (v. 11).

The revelation given to Nathan is one of the most significant in the Old Testament as it introduces us to God's covenant with David and his promises, which are not just to his family but to the whole world.

The promises here concerning David's 'offspring' refer, of course, to Solomon, who builds the temple, but they reach far beyond him to a future son of David—the Messiah. Their fulfilment is seen in the mission of Jesus Christ, born of David's line, and the one who came to introduce the kingdom of God in all its fullness.

Mary herself recognized the fulfilment of this prophecy as the angel spoke to her about the child she was to bear: 'The Lord God will give him the throne of his father David, and he will reign over the house of Jacob forever; his kingdom will never end' (Luke 1:32–33).

The significance of all this for David is the awareness that there is a kingdom greater than his own—the kingdom of God. For us it lies in the realization that Jesus is our king and our allegiance belongs to him alone.

Prayer

Reign in me, sovereign Lord.

TH

David's prayer

Then King David went in and sat before the Lord, and he said: 'Who am I, O Sovereign Lord, and what is my family, that you have brought me this far? And as if this were not enough in your sight, O Sovereign Lord, you have also spoken about the future of the house of your servant. Is this your usual way of dealing with people, O Sovereign Lord? … O Lord Almighty, God of Israel, you have revealed this to your servant, saying, "I will build a house for you." So your servant has found courage to offer you this prayer. O Sovereign Lord, you are God! Your words are trustworthy, and you have promised these good things to your servant. Now be pleased to bless the house of your servant, that it may continue for ever in your sight; for you, O Sovereign Lord, have spoken, and with your blessing the house of your servant will be blessed forever.'

Overwhelmed by the revelation given through the prophet Nathan, David finds a place to be still and pours out his heart to God. It provides a wonderful example of how to talk to God in prayer. We can identify four strands within his prayer. First, there is the grace of God (vv. 18–21). David reflects on the fact that he is undeserving of such blessing, but acknowledges that God always deals with us on the basis of undeserved kindness. Second, there is the greatness of God (vv. 22–24). David considers the mighty deeds of God in the past to remind himself that he has the power to bring his purposes to fulfilment. Third, there is the glory of God (vv. 25–26). David seeks a good reputation not for himself but for his God, so that people will recognize it as God's doing. Finally, there is the goodness of God (vv. 27–29). David trusts that God will be true to his word and bring the promises to pass, so that his family and future generations will be blessed.

Throughout the prayer David's petition is addressed to the 'Sovereign Lord'. The title reminds us that God is in control, he rules over the affairs of the earth and will most certainly bring his purposes to pass. David's confidence —and our own—rests in a God who truly reigns and in whose sovereignty we can trust.

Prayer

Lord, you alone are worthy to be praised!

TH

Silas... who's he?

In contemplating the beginnings of the Church immediately after the death and resurrection of Jesus, we tend to focus on the life and ministry of Paul. Luke, the author of Acts, encourages us to do this and, indeed, there is no doubt that without Paul the story of the Early Church would have been very different. Some commentators would have us believe that Paul founded Christianity, in as much as it was his work that established an organized Church and a way of mission and his letters provided the earliest guidance on Christian living. While we may not want to characterize his role quite like this, it is very difficult to remove Paul from the picture the early propagation of Christ's ministry and purpose. It was Paul's understanding of and ability to communicate Christ's message that achieved so much in the years after the resurrection.

Yet, Paul did not act alone—there were others who should share some of the credit. For Luke, writing Acts, these others are less significant, but some do get a mention from time to time and, even in the little space he gives them, we encounter men and women of faith, integrity, courage and determination. Some of them possessed qualities of diplomacy, tolerance and tact that Paul himself lacked. One such person was Silas, also known as Silvanus.

These next two weeks, we shall be looking at some of the events described in Acts in which Silas appears, as either a significant or a subsidiary character. Sometimes he—and, to some extent, Timothy, too—are recorded as being present when things happen to or are done by Paul. On other occasions, we read or infer that Silas is asked to do something different, sometimes elsewhere. So, while Silas rarely appears in the foreground, it is clear that his contribution as a companion of Paul and as a minister in his own right is significant. We also know that, after Paul's ministry was over, Silas worked with Peter, acting as his letter bearer to churches dispersed throughout Asia Minor (see 1 Peter 5:12). Compared with Paul, information about Silas is thin on the ground, but his strength of character, commitment and obedience glow through the pages of Acts and it is by that light that we travel with Silas and draw inspiration from his ministry.

Gordon Giles

Silas is chosen

Then the apostles and the elders, with the consent of the whole church, decided to choose men from among their members and to send them to Antioch with Paul and Barnabas. They sent Judas called Barsabbas, and Silas, leaders among the brothers, with the following letter: 'The brothers, both the apostles and the elders, to the believers of Gentile origin in Antioch and Syria and Cilicia, greetings.'

There are many ways to make decisions: science, law and democracy all have their different procedures. In matters of faith and discipleship, we speak of 'discernment' and, ever since the time of Christ, the Church has sought to discern the will of God, transmitted by the Holy Spirit.

In this passage, we hear of two decisions made by the apostles—the remaining original disciples of Christ—along with elders who have been subsequently appointed. First, they decide to send others to go with Paul and Barnabas, who presumably have a say in the matter. Then they must decide whom to send. How do they reach these decisions? We are not told: Luke is more interested in the result of the decision than in how it is reached. After Judas Iscariot betrayed Jesus and killed himself (Matthew 27:5), Matthias was chosen as a result of casting lots (Acts 1:26). Nowadays, we may well have qualms about a procedure that is so closely linked to gambling, but we should remember how common it was in Greco-Roman culture. Furthermore, there is no evidence that Silas and Judas Barsabbas were elected in this way as the uncontroversial account of the decision to send them and those particular men implies that they were appointed by common consensus (perhaps at Paul's bidding).

Nowadays, different denominations have different procedures for appointing leaders. Candidates usually go through a discernment process involving interviews, even psychological and academic tests. Senior leaders are elected by the majority, appointed by government or even chosen by secret ballot. It seems a long way from the call of Silas! Yet, the Holy Spirit can cope with it all and, even 2000 years on, God still calls men and women to his service through the ministry of Christ's body on earth, the universal Church.

Reflection

Jesus calls me and sends me that I may do his will.

GG

Letter of commendation

'Since we have heard that certain persons who have gone out from us, though with no instructions from us, have said things to disturb you and have unsettled your minds, we have decided unanimously to choose representatives and send them to you, along with our beloved Barnabas and Paul, who have risked their lives for the sake of our Lord Jesus Christ. We have therefore sent Judas and Silas, who themselves will tell you the same things by word of mouth.'

Judas and Silas are diplomats in both the political and the missionary sense. They are 'ambassadors for Christ', to act and speak in a way worthy of their calling, but they also have a delicate role in terms of Christian unity. The letter of introduction from the apostles and elders is polite but forthright, containing a rebuke and a show of concern for the body politic of the wider Church. Word has come that the Judaizers (those who want Christian converts to become Jews first) have claimed an apostolic authority that the apostles and elders do not endorse, so they are sending two of their best people to deal sensitively but graciously with the situation.

The problem was almost inevitable and the very nature and context of Jesus' earthly ministry was always going to mean that this issue would need to be resolved. Do pagan converts need to become Jewish, too, or, to put it differently, should the men be circumcised? Whether you are male or female, you can imagine what an off-putting thought that would be to an adult male. Those contemplating turning to the Lord Jesus Christ would not be helped to do so by those Christian leaders who insisted that they undergo a physical ritual that is certainly not for the squeamish!

It is hard for us today, who take the universality of Christ's message for granted, to think of Judaism being the doorway to Christianity, such that a Gentile had to follow its laws to pass through it, painful and humiliating as that would have been for them. For Paul and Silas it was a real issue, but they resolved it once and for all. Christians need not become Jewish to be accepted, nor do they need any physical badge in order do so as they are called to 'faith working through love' (Galatians 5:6).

Prayer

Lord, we are marked by your call.
Send us in your service. Amen

GG

Mission accomplished

So they were sent off and went down to Antioch. When they gathered the congregation together, they delivered the letter. When its members read it, they rejoiced at the exhortation. Judas and Silas, who were themselves prophets, said much to encourage and strengthen the believers. After they had been there for some time, they were sent off in peace by the believers to those who had sent them. But Paul and Barnabas remained in Antioch, and there, with many others, they taught and proclaimed the word of the Lord.

Having considered how unpleasant circumcision would have seemed to new, non-Jewish converts, it is perhaps no surprise that the message from the apostles went down well. Nevertheless, Luke tells us that Silas and Judas are prophets and great encouragers. They did far more than simply read out and endorse a letter from head office.

We can only speculate about what they said to encourage the congregation they addressed, but we are probably safe in imagining a positive atmosphere in which, perhaps diplomatically, they thanked the congregation for hosting and welcoming them, read out the letter, then gave accounts of the work of the Spirit in places they had recently visited. They probably also expounded scripture and recalled stories and the acts of Jesus from Gospels as yet unwritten.

We can imagine this happening because today visiting preachers and leaders do likewise. When someone new comes to preach in your church, how do you react? There is a sense in which it is quite exciting as a new voice, a different style or personality is encountered. In many churches, the same group of people preach week in, week out, but a visitor can create a buzz of anticipation. To be fair, though, not all visitors reward that anticipation and can sometimes disappoint an expectant congregation! Not so for Silas and Judas, who certainly left a good impression. They were invited to stay a while and, even when they left, Paul and Barnabas remained welcome. When they got home, they must have delighted those who sent them with the news that their mission, in every sense of the word, had been accomplished.

Prayer

Lord, may we accomplish our missions with compassion and goodwill. Amen

GG

ACTS 15:36–40 (NRSV)

Parting company

After some days Paul said to Barnabas, 'Come, let us return and visit the believers in every city where we proclaimed the word of the Lord and see how they are doing.' Barnabas wanted to take with them John called Mark. But Paul decided not to take with them one who had deserted them in Pamphylia and had not accompanied them in the work. The disagreement became so sharp that they parted company; Barnabas took Mark with him and sailed away to Cyprus. But Paul chose Silas and set out, the believers commending him to the grace of the Lord.

In a sense, Paul is the hero of the Acts of the Apostles. Here we read how he parted company with Barnabas and John Mark, who then went to Cyprus, away from the main plot of the story, which concerns the acts of Paul. As he is the central figure, his colleagues pale into apparent insignificance, which is frustrating for us and a little unfair to them. Judas Barsabbas does not get a mention ever again and we are merely told that Silas is sufficiently valued by Paul to be selected as his companion.

Paul has a reason for not trusting John Mark and, undoubtedly, with his characteristic tenaciousness, will not be persuaded by Barnabas, who probably made a good case for giving John Mark a second chance. We can imagine Paul and Barnabas having a row about this and Paul saying something like, 'If you trust him, take him with you'. This altercation tells us about Silas, for it seems that he is everything Paul thinks John Mark is not. Silas is loyal, reliable, courageous, trustworthy, supportive and, as we have already heard, something of a prophet and a preacher.

It is worth noticing the original cause of the dispute that leaves Silas with Paul. It is a secondary disagreement: Barnabas is happy to visit churches they have established, so, as a consequence of their falling out, we can presume that twice as many churches were visited and encouraged. God moves in mysterious ways, as the saying goes, and advantages came out of even what may otherwise seem like a shameful argument.

Prayer

Lord, give us grace to treat with respect those with whom we disagree and to always act to enhance your glory. Amen

GG

Slave to fortune

One day, as we were going to the place of prayer, we met a slave girl who had a spirit of divination and brought her owners a great deal of money by fortune-telling. While she followed Paul and us, she would cry out, 'These men are slaves of the Most High God, who proclaim to you a way of salvation.' She kept doing this for many days. But Paul, very much annoyed, turned and said to the spirit, 'I order you in the name of Jesus Christ to come out of her.' And it came out that very hour.

The reason Luke's Acts follows Paul and not Barnabas is quite simple: he travelled with Paul and Silas and, sometimes, as in this passage, he writes as an eye-witness. We can safely assume that he saw this incident with the slave girl. He does not mention Silas by name, but we know that he was there too because of what happens next: as a result of this miracle, Paul and Silas are thrown in prison.

One thing can so easily lead to another, sometimes with unpleasant or dangerous consequences. Paul does not like sorcery or fortunetelling, nor what here is called 'divination'. The slave girl—either by divination or, perhaps, by following Paul and Silas—has worked out who they are and whom they serve. By following them and blurting it out, she is being tactless and unhelpful, perhaps even endangering them. So, Paul acts in a way that is both defensive and proac-

tive. He silences the annoying voice and, in doing so, releases the girl from the thrall of the spirit. What he does has a double advantage, with both short- and long-term consequences.

What the girl says is true: Paul and Silas are speaking of salvation and, even if the source of her gift of discernment was unacceptable to them, having her as a human placard might have been quite useful. But Paul and Silas do not want to be associated in any way with the suspicious and unchristian magic she uses. Even though she is effectively telling the truth, they do her a favour, both freeing and silencing her. However, they are not going to get away with it, as we shall see.

Prayer

Lord, lead us into truth with your light alone. Amen

GG

Paul and Silas are arrested

But when her owners saw that their hope of making money was gone, they seized Paul and Silas and dragged them into the marketplace before the authorities... They said, 'These men are disturbing our city; they are Jews and are advocating customs that are not lawful for us as Romans to adopt or observe.' The crowd joined in attacking them, and the magistrates had them stripped of their clothing and ordered them to be beaten with rods... They threw them into prison and ordered the jailer to keep them securely... He put them in the innermost cell and fastened their feet in the stocks.

Money motivates many things. In this case, the fact that Paul and Silas have deprived the slave's owners of a nice income has made them angry and caused them to seek revenge. As is often the case, even today, the cause of their complaint is not the real cause of their resentment. As undermining someone's income is not a crime in itself, they have to pursue a different charge and so they come up with the accusation that Paul and Silas (who are, in fact, Roman citizens) are causing a disturbance and advocating illegal behaviour. Their charge is effective and it leads to Paul and Silas' immediate incarceration without much of a trial. Merely accusing someone can heap on them considerable inconvenience or danger. Paul and Silas' detractors knew exactly how to get their revenge!

Now Paul and Silas find themselves up before a magistrate. He is influenced by the jeering crowd and, while he may have felt strongly about the case, it is also possible that he understood perfectly what was going on. Perhaps taking the easy way out, he read the mood of the angry crowd and gave them what they wanted: a flogging.

The situation is not so different from the scene in Jerusalem years earlier when the Roman governor Pontius Pilate gave way to a manipulative mob and had Jesus whipped and crucified. That connection may not occur to us immediately now, but I suspect that the painful and humiliating similarity of their punishments may well have occurred to Paul and Silas and possibly sustained them during what must have been a time of extreme hardship.

Prayer

Lord, give comfort to all who are persecuted, hurt or humiliated for your sake. Amen

GG

39

Earthquake!

About midnight Paul and Silas were praying and singing hymns to God, and the prisoners were listening to them. Suddenly there was an earthquake, so violent that the foundations of the prison were shaken; and immediately all the doors were opened and everyone's chains were unfastened. When the jailer woke up and saw the prison doors wide open, he drew his sword and was about to kill himself, since he supposed that the prisoners had escaped. But Paul shouted in a loud voice, 'Do not harm yourself, for we are all here.'

Paul and Silas were having a tough time, having been beaten and put in the stocks, which would very quickly have become very uncomfortable. Unable to move properly and nursing wounds, they started to sing hymns. They did this for three reasons: to boost their spirits and those of their fellow prisoners, to take their minds off the pain and slow passage of time, and to witness to their faith. While some find it hard to pray or sing when God seems to have abandoned them, Silas and Paul were clearly in no doubt that God was with them and so they praised him still.

Then there was an earthquake. It was not a particularly surprising event for that region, but it was strong enough to shake the building, open the cell doors and break the prisoners' chains. Silas and Paul were free, but they did not run away, which we would probably have expected them to do. While lesser men would have legged it, they considered their jailer.

Have we ever been faced with a similar choice? Thankfully, few of us will have endured the trauma of flogging, prison and earthquakes, but the temptation to look entirely to our own advantage when good fortune strikes remains very real today. Paul and Silas suffered much and then events took an unexpected turn for the better. They kept their dignity in the face of both, however, and did not simply focus on their own concerns.

We must not forget the divine dimension in all this. God protected them and then brought about their release. Thus, it was their absolute trust in him that enabled them to remain calm and focused in trouble and in joy and makes them examples to Christians in any age.

Prayer

Lord, give us grace to trust you whatever happens. Amen

GG

Calling for light

The jailer called for lights, and rushing in, he fell down trembling before Paul and Silas. Then he brought them outside and said, 'Sirs, what must I do to be saved?' They answered, 'Believe on the Lord Jesus, and you will be saved, you and your household.' They spoke the word of the Lord to him and to all who were in his house. At the same hour of the night he took them and washed their wounds; then he and his entire family were baptized without delay. He brought them up into the house and set food before them; and he and his entire household rejoiced that he had become a believer in God.

Even if the jailer wasn't joining in with the hymnsinging, he seems to have been inspired by it. We saw yesterday how Paul and Silas witnessed to their faith by not only singing and praying but also remaining calm and in their consideration for the jailer, such that they effectively saved his life. Now comes the spiritual reward for all of them: the jailer discovers Christ as his saviour and Paul and Silas can delight in the prospect. Such experiences are, after all, the desire and purpose of their preaching and teaching. Given the circumstances, this must have been a particularly special one to remember and give thanks for.

It was a dramatic conversion for the jailer, the like of which is unusual even today. Did you have such a conversion experience yourself, when your life was so completely turned around that you can remember not being a Christian one day and being a new creation the next? Not everyone does, nor is it necessarily better or more holy to be able to do so. For some, the calling to faith is a seed that grows and blossoms slowly.

Nevertheless, whether your calling came in a big bang, as it did for the jailer, or was forged in extremis or quietly over a longer period, becoming a stable part of your being, for all of us there is that delight when the illumination we and others seek becomes the glow of faith.

Reflection

Many people, like the jailer, are trapped in prisons of their own making, but only have to call for light to receive freedom and enlightenment.

GG

The pace of change

After Paul and Silas had passed through Amphipolis and Apollonia, they came to Thessalonica, where there was a synagogue of the Jews. And Paul went in, as was his custom, and on three sabbath days argued with them from the scriptures, explaining and proving that it was necessary for the Messiah to suffer and to rise from the dead, and saying, 'This is the Messiah, Jesus whom I am proclaiming to you.' Some of them were persuaded and joined Paul and Silas, as did a great many of the devout Greeks and not a few of the leading women.

There is a confused historical tradition that distinguishes between Silas and Silvanus. They are, in fact, the same person, as Silvanus is the Latinate version of Silas. Some reference books suggest that Silvanus ultimately became bishop of Thessalonica, and it is from Silas' association with the city that the confusion arises.

Silas visited Thessalonica, for sure. Indeed, when Paul wrote to the Thessalonians, he mentioned Silvanus (Silas): 'Paul, Silvanus, and Timothy, To the church of the Thessalonians' (1 Thessalonians 1:1; 2 Thessalonians 1:1). The three leaders sent their good wishes to those whom they had met, seen, converted and ultimately left behind. Paul, Silas and Timothy must have had some memories of their visit and the joy they felt when their mission yielded fruit.

They must have been pleased and eventually not surprised to see Gentile Greeks turning to Christ, too. In this much they were, as Paul was to put it later, 'all things to all people' (1 Corinthians 9:22) for we learn that in this Greek city there were not only important men but also 'leading women', some of whom became Christians. That fact is important, for when leaders convert, many follow and things change. It was Emperor Constantine's mother Helena who encouraged him to become a Christian, and his conversion transformed the history and faith of the Western world. Silas and Paul visited Thessalonica three centuries earlier, but their visit and the people they persuaded and encouraged set the pace for worldwide spiritual change.

Prayer

Father, we remember with admiration and gratitude all those courageous early runners of faith's race. May we emulate them and strive for the crown of righteousness. Amen

GG

Belief in Beroea

That very night the believers sent Paul and Silas off to Beroea; and when they arrived, they went to the Jewish synagogue. These Jews were more receptive than those in Thessalonica, for they welcomed the message very eagerly and examined the scriptures every day to see whether these things were so. Many of them therefore believed, including not a few Greek women and men of high standing.

Paul, Timothy and Silas move on from Thessalonica to Beroea, where they get a better reception. Beroea is situated at the foot of Mount Bermios in Macedonia, but today it has the Greek name Veria. According to the *Apostolic Constitutions* (VII, 46), Onesimus, the slave referred to by Philemon in his letter, became its first bishop. In due course, the episcopal see fell under that of Thessalonica. Today, Veria has about 35,000 inhabitants.

It must have been rewarding, and a relief, to find fertile ground for the gospel in Beroea. Luke tells us that the folk in the synagogue were persuaded by examining scripture, checking what they had heard. This reveals that Paul and Silas continued to take the approach that Jesus was the long-expected Messiah, the one to whom the Jewish Bible pointed. We are reminded of Jesus on the road to Emmaus, explaining the scriptures as they related to himself (Luke 24:27). This approach made a lot of sense at the time, but it was less inspiring to non-Jews.

Today, preachers and missionaries do not generally make a great deal of the Jewish prophetic heritage relating to the Messiah, except perhaps at Christmas carol services, where it gains poignancy because we are celebrating the nativity. For us today, whose intellectual and cultural heritage is more Gentile than Jewish, the idea that Jesus fulfils Jewish prophecy often passes unnoticed. We are perhaps more persuaded by the hope of heaven and the mercy and love of God revealed in Christ. However, we must never lose sight of Christianity's Jewish heritage—and not just at the level that Jesus was a Jew among Jews. We should appreciate that Jewish scripture (our Old Testament) points Jews and Gentiles alike to the reality and meaning of his coming.

Prayer

Jesus, you reveal yourself in history; be alive in our hearts. Amen

GG

Troublemakers

But when the Jews of Thessalonica learned that the word of God had been proclaimed by Paul in Beroea as well, they came there too, to stir up and incite the crowds. Then the believers immediately sent Paul away to the coast, but Silas and Timothy remained behind. Those who conducted Paul brought him as far as Athens; and after receiving instructions to have Silas and Timothy join him as soon as possible, they left him.

The success of the apostles' preaching in Beroea upset the zealous Jews of Thessalonica, who came specifically to cause trouble. In our age, we see this kind of behaviour among football hooligans, political activists and rioters. Sadly, there are people who will travel to be part of the action, where action means disturbance, even violence. G8 summits and international football matches attract both activists and hooligans who, it seems, are more committed to troublemaking than to a cause or team.

Getting inside this mindset is not always easy and it is tempting not to bother. It is much easier to dismiss those who oppose us or stir up trouble against us. Nowadays, it is not so much members of other faiths who are anti-Christian as those who profess no faith and consider Christianity (and other forms of faith) as having a negative impact on society. It is rather ironic that advocates of radical atheism cite religious intolerance as an example of the evils of faith, but engage in a polemic that itself often comes across as insulting, ill-informed and philosophically weak.

Back in Beroea, Paul is packed off to the coast when trouble looms, but Silas and Timothy bravely remain to face the music and defend the cause. Soon they also leave— forced out by the bigotry and nastiness of the Thessalonian rabble-rousers. It must have been difficult and depressing to confront those whose opinions were aggressive and whose minds were closed. Rational argument or discussion with such people is seldom possible and rarely fruitful, so we must suppose that Silas and Timothy did their best, then moved on with dignity and integrity.

Prayer

Lord, when others revile and discredit your word of truth and love, protect and inspire those in your service. Amen

GG

Too busy for friends?

Every sabbath he [Paul] would argue in the synagogue and would try to convince Jews and Greeks. When Silas and Timothy arrived from Macedonia, Paul was occupied with proclaiming the word, testifying to the Jews that the Messiah was Jesus.

There are two sides to every story and this brief mention of Silas and Timothy arriving to find Paul pre-occupied can be seen in two ways. First, they might have been distressed to arrive and find that Paul was busy, even if it was in pursuit of the gospel. Friends have value, too, and relationships are worth putting some effort into. Have you ever called on friends, only to find them busy? They let you in, but then return to the telephone conversation they were having or to the computer to finish the e-mail they're writing, saying, 'Hello, do come in, I'm just in the middle of something—I'll be with you in a minute.' Then, many minutes later, they return and you finally feel welcome. Timothy and Silas may have felt a bit like that. We can only hope that Paul eventually did take time out to greet them and spend some time with his fellow workers and friends.

Equally, however, we have no evidence that Silas and Timothy were annoyed that Paul was busy. Indeed, they may have been encouraged. Whatever they felt, they knew Paul well enough not to be surprised. We can imagine Silas and Timothy saying to one another, 'We've arrived at last and Paul's out preaching. Perhaps we'll catch up with him later. That Paul, he never gives up, you've got to admire him.' And admire him they did, of course.

How was it for Paul? Have you ever had good friends turn up and simply been too busy to welcome them? It's awkward because you would love to sit down and chat, but you just can't. Unannounced visitors always understand, but they are disappointed nonetheless. Have you ever been so busy doing the Lord's work that you don't have time for friends or family? I have and I wonder what Paul or Silas might say about it. I also wonder what our Lord would want us to do about it.

Prayer

Lord, help us find time for the work of the gospel, both in witnessing out and about and caring at home.
Amen

GG

From Macedonia to Corinth

When [those at the synagogue] opposed and reviled [Paul], in protest he shook the dust from his clothes and said to them, 'Your blood be on your own heads! I am innocent. From now on I will go to the Gentiles.' Then he left the synagogue and went to the house of a man named Titius Justus, a worshipper of God... He stayed there a year and six months, teaching the word of God among them.

Paul was having quite a hard time when Silas and Timothy arrived in Corinth, which, to us as readers of the New Testament, is a key location for the apostle's ministry and correspondence. As a result, like Paul, we gain first-hand knowledge of the lifestyle and attitudes of the Corinthian Christians, many of which crop up in the letters passing between the Corinthian church leaders and their founder. The issues include marriage, the conduct of the eucharist, spiritual gifts, idolatry and lifestyle. In 2 Corinthians, Paul specifically encourages them to be generous to the Jerusalem Christians, using the Macedonians' generosity as an example (see ch. 9). Thus, Silas and Timothy have arrived from Macedonia, where they have been encouraging, even thanking, those generous Christians.

What they discover on their arrival is not so encouraging: soon Paul is being 'reviled and opposed' by the Jewish contingent and so decides to focus his attentions on the Greek, Gentile population, to whom he will eventually write the letters known as 1 and 2 Corinthians. Titius Justus and his friends are more receptive and Paul spends 18 months with them, even though his letters reveal that he needs to keep nurturing them from afar!

Silas and Timothy's reaction to Paul's abandonment of his Jewish mission in Corinth is not recorded, but it is clear that Paul was frustrated, upset and angry by the opposition he met and it is likely that Silas and Timothy shared his feelings. It is interesting to speculate as to whether or not, in today's results-driven culture, it is even harder to acknowledge that faith-sharing efforts appear to be fruitless. However, such an outcome is not to be attributed to a failure of faith or lack of skill, but, rather, to a sign that here and now it is not part of God's plan for universal salvation.

Prayer

Lord, give us the grace to witness through good and ill. Amen

GG

What happened to Silas?

After staying [in Corinth] for a considerable time, Paul said farewell to the believers and sailed for Syria, accompanied by Priscilla and Aquila... When they reached Ephesus, he left them there, but first he himself went into the synagogue and had a discussion with the Jews. When they asked him to stay longer, he declined; but on taking leave of them, he said, 'I will return to you, if God wills.' Then he set sail from Ephesus.

If we assume that Silas had not moved on during the year that Paul spent in Corinth, this must have been when they parted company, although Silas is not actually named here. Paul had found himself in trouble again, hauled up before Gallio, the proconsul of Achaia, who dismissed the case against him. Another man, a synagogue official called Sosthenes, was beaten in a mindless act of frustration by the crowd (see vv. 12–17). There is no reference to Silas or Timothy in that account, so we must presume that they had either already moved on by then or managed to keep out of that dispute.

So, what happened to Silas? One tradition holds that, while Paul left Corinth, Silas did not, ultimately becoming the bishop of Corinth. When Paul reached Ephesus, he wrote at least part of his second letter to the Corinthians, reminding them that they knew Silas and would remember him for his most affirming preaching of the gospel:

'For the Son of God... whom we proclaimed among you, Silvanus and Timothy and I, was not "Yes and No"; but in him it is always "Yes"' (2 Corinthians 1:19). As we have seen, Silvanus and Silas are the same person, respected among the Corinthians as someone who helped them discover that God was unequivocally on their side.

Silas' final fate is not known. Some say he joined Peter in northern Asia, as he is mentioned in Peter's first letter: 'Through Silvanus, whom I consider a faithful brother, I have written this short letter to encourage you...' (1 Peter 5:12). Silas clearly continued an itinerant ministry after his separation from Paul, whose fate, it appears, he did not share. Tradition has it that he died in Macedonia.

Prayer
Lord, thank you for the witness and ministry of Silas, your unsung servant of the gospel.

GG

Words of love

Our first experience of love precedes all words. Whether our conception was welcome or not, we spend our first few months of life in a warm womb in which every single one of our needs is met. In those crucial weeks we are being knit together secretly in ways none but God can know. We are then born into this world as a unique human being and also born into a family, a community, a culture, a history and a future.

So, we begin these two weeks of reflections with a contemplation of God's ancient and eternal love for his people. Though all images are inadequate as means of capturing the reality of God, the image of parenting can nevertheless help us to explore some aspects of what it means to be loved by God. We discover God as the origin of our being and acknowledge God as the loving parent who is continuously in labour, striving to bring to birth the person we truly are, guiding us, restraining us, gathering us up in our weakness and celebrating the fullness of everything that we can become.

As we grow, the love we experience and share is expressed in both words and actions. In the life of Jesus, we see God's words of love shaped and expressed in human form. We continue our journey by listening to what Jesus teaches us about the true nature of love, reminding us that, to follow him, we need to 'come and see' for ourselves who he really is for us. We need to see each other through his eyes, we need to trust him and learn from him how to make 'decisions for love' in particular situations, even though our feelings may be far from loving.

Finally, we hear the expression of love in Jesus' own final prayer for his friends and we can let that prayer reverberate through our own hearts as surely as it did through the hearts of the first disciples.

A child learns to speak by hearing others and then imitating what has been heard. We learn the language of God's love in the same way—first, by listening to God's words of love to us and then by becoming words of love to each other and the world.

Margaret Silf

Love—the first word of all

O Lord, you have searched me and known me. You know when I sit down and when I rise up; you discern my thoughts from far away. You search out my path and my lying down, and are acquainted with all my ways. Even before a word is on my tongue, O Lord, you know it completely... For it was you who formed my inward parts; you knit me together in my mother's womb... My frame was not hidden from you, when I was being made in secret, intricately woven in the depths of the earth. Your eyes beheld my unformed substance. In your book were written all the days that were formed for me, when none of them as yet existed.

People say that grandparenting is even better than parenting. Maybe it's because the older generations tend to have more time to simply 'be' with the young. My own experience of grandparenthood is only just beginning. In fact, at the time of writing, the expected little one is still unborn, but already I am noticing some unexpected reactions. I realize that I am aware of this tiny human presence slowly unfurling within my daughter in a way that I was not when I was pregnant myself.

Then, perhaps, there were too many anxieties. Would I be capable of looking after a new life? How would I juggle motherhood and work? Now, a generation further on, I find myself reflecting with the psalmist that a new human being is being shaped and knitted together in secret. Cells are dividing and multiplying, each becoming what it is destined to be, a minuscule particle of a new creation. This little person is growing, quietly and without any help from us, and he or she is already known to God— was known to God since the beginning of time in ways we shall never understand.

That thought renders me speechless with wonder: a new child is coming into being, one with whom I shall have a special, unique relationship, one whom I already feel I know and love, in some still hidden way, and one whom God already knows and loves completely.

Reflection

Every new life is a unique particle of God's dream unfolding on planet earth. May we cherish our little ones. They are born out of and into God's eternal love.

MS

Love's labour

For a long time I have held my peace, I have kept still and restrained myself; now I will cry out like a woman in labour, I will gasp and pant. I will lay waste mountains and hills, and dry up all their herbage; I will turn the rivers into islands, and dry up the pools. I will lead the blind by a road they do not know, by paths they have not known I will guide them. I will turn the darkness before them into light, the rough places into level ground. These are the things I will do, and I will not forsake them.

What is conceived in love is nevertheless brought to birth in agonizing pain and sheer hard labour. Today we are reminded of a God who is constantly labouring to bring to birth the sons and daughters for whom he has longed for all eternity. We only need to look around us to see what a difficult birth this is. The world seems to be crying out in terror and lashing out at itself in rage. Becoming the people we are destined by God to become seems to provoke huge resistance.

When labour pains begin and the baby is relentlessly squeezed out of the protective cocoon of the womb, it 'loses' everything: its home, food supply, entire comfort zone and even—apparently—its mother. From the baby's point of view, birth seems to be the very opposite of a loving act, yet it is, in fact, the first act of love we give to our children. We set them free to live and both child and mother scream out their anguish.

Today we hear how God gives birth to us, also in anguish. Just listen, however to the promise: out of the darkness of the womb God will lead us into light, just as a baby is born into the light of day. Like a loving parent, God here undertakes to lead us, his blind infants, along the roads of life we cannot yet either see or predict.

Reflection

Parenthood is one of the few relationships that is for ever. Whatever happens, once your baby has been born, you can never stop being its parent. God gives his word to us, too: this is for ever; we will never be forsaken.

MS

Love's leading reins

When Israel was a child, I loved him, and out of Egypt I called my son. The more I called them, the more they went from me; they kept sacrificing to the Baals, and offering incense to idols. Yet it was I who taught Ephraim to walk, I took them up in my arms; but they did not know that I healed them. I led them with cords of human kindness, with bands of love. I was to them like those who lift infants to their cheeks. I bent down to them and fed them.

No one who has ever had dealings with small children will forget the trials of the so-called 'terrible twos'. As our little ones increase in self-awareness and have a growing desire for independence (for which, of course, they are by no means ready) we encounter the archetypal clash of wills between the growing child and the caring parent. It is time for the 'leading reins'.

For the child, the reins are clearly a restraint, imposed on it by its unreasonable elders for the sole purpose of frustrating its spirit of adventure. For the parents they are the means of safeguarding the child from all the dangers of a world full of risks. The one who imposes the restraints is also the one who holds the little one close and bends down to comfort and feed it.

God's toddlers (ourselves included) are no less forceful in asserting their autonomy. What begins with the terrible twos goes on to become the tumultuous teens. I remember a moment of insight I had once while swimming in our local pool. As I pushed myself off from the side of the pool, with some force, I thought about how my teenage daughter had sometimes seemed to be pushing against me with that kind of force. Then it dawned on me that she had not been pushing me away, but pushing herself off into the next phase of her life. After that I didn't take the pushes so personally!

Today's reading reminds us that, just as a river needs a riverbank, so love flows most fully through the channels of caring restraint.

Reflection

May God give us the wisdom to know when to restrain and when to liberate. May we welcome God's restraints on us as signs of his love.

MS

Love's longing

For surely I know the plans I have for you, says the Lord, plans for your welfare and not for harm, to give you a future with hope. Then when you call upon me and come and pray to me, I will hear you. When you search for me, you will find me; if you seek me with all your heart, I will let you find me, says the Lord, and I will restore your fortunes and gather you from all the nations and all the places where I have driven you, says the Lord, and I will bring you back to the place from which I sent you into exile.

Teenagers invariably see their parents or guardians as agents of opposition, forever devising ways to prevent them from doing their own thing. If you were to ask many Christians what they think is meant by 'God's will', they would probably say that, whatever it is, it is almost certainly diametrically opposed to our own desires. We often project our teenage thinking on to God and, when we do, we miss the point rather seriously.

I remain truly grateful to those who helped me to understand that, at the deepest level of my being, my own desire is at one with God's desire for me. God's desire, like the desire of a human parent, is always for our welfare and our greater good. It may clash with our superficial wants and wishes—just as the parent's loving concern for a child may appear to thwart the child's immediate aspirations—but, at the deepest level, God desires that we experience the fullness of life in every possible way.

When our own choices and reactions are in tune with God's deepest level of desiring, we will sense a resonance with his desire to love us. When we are living from the shallower reaches of our being, we will detect, if we are honest, a dissonance within ourselves, an unease that warns us that we are going astray from our true selves.

Today, however, God's word of love promises us that not only is he constantly striving for our good but also he is always waiting to bring us home to our true selves and to him.

Reflection
God plans to lead us to the fullest possible good—and his plans will prevail.

MS

Love's gentleness

Here is my servant, whom I uphold, my chosen, in whom my soul delights; I have put my spirit upon him; he will bring forth justice to the nations. He will not cry or lift up his voice, or make it heard in the street; a bruised reed he will not break, and a dimly burning wick he will not quench; he will faithfully bring forth justice. He will not grow faint or be crushed until he has established justice in the earth; and the coastlands wait for his teaching.

Striving for our children's greatest good can seem like a constant struggle. For us human beings it can often feel as if it is a losing battle. They resist our well-intentioned guidance. They insist on doing things their way. They come unstuck. They get lost. They drift into dangerous currents and get out of their depth. They may be badly hurt by life or betrayed in their personal relationships. What do we do then?

One March morning, when the daffodils were just coming into bloom and, at the same time, the worst of the spring storms was raging, I stooped to pick up a broken daffodil that was lying on the grass. It had been snapped off by the wind. I brought it indoors, put it in a vase, gave it some water and, in return, it filled several days with joy. I wish I could say that I have always been so gentle in my parenting, but the incident brought to mind the promise in today's passage from Isaiah. God will not break the bruised reed or snuff out the faltering candle. What a promise! What words of love! If I bother to pick up and tend to a broken daffodil, how much more will God do for his children?

The worst storms often coincide with the most critical seasons of growth and change. Sooner or later, each of us feels like a bruised reed, helpless against the buffeting, or a faltering flame, prey to the cold draughts of life, events that leave us reeling. We know, though, that we can put our trust in the God of love.

Reflection

God will not crush me when I am down, but will gather me up, again and again and again. He will do all this in silence and in stillness.

MS

Love overflowing

You shall eat in plenty and be satisfied, and praise the name of the Lord your God, who has dealt wondrously with you. And my people shall never again be put to shame. You shall know that I am in the midst of Israel, and that I, the Lord, am your God and there is no other. And my people shall never again be put to shame. Then afterward I will pour out my spirit on all flesh; your sons and daughters shall prophesy, your old men shall dream dreams, and your young men shall see visions. Even on the male and female slaves, in those days, I will pour out my spirit.

God's many words of love are not only about maintenance, about soothing our hurts and guiding our steps. There is more, much more! Just listen to today's words and promise. For a start, there is going to be a feast. The very moving film *Babette's Feast* recounts how a woman who has almost nothing unexpectedly comes into a small fortune and blows it all on a magnificent feast for the whole community. It's a completely over-the-top affair, with no expense spared. The finest food and drink is brought in from all over and served in spectacular style. Everyone is bowled over.

God's words of love today are like that—so completely and outrageously over the top that our jaws drop. It's as though Christmas is over, we have unwrapped the last of our presents and, then, on Boxing Day, we discover an extra parcel that we didn't notice

was there. That extra gift is so great it can't even be wrapped but has to be poured out and there is no end to its abundance.

God's 'more' is nothing less than this: humanity shall become so deeply and fully aware of the mystery of love in which it is grounded that our joy will overflow its banks, flooding each one of us, without exception, with dreams and visions of who we can become, as God's Spirit flows through creation.

Reflection

Just when we think we have feasted until we can feast no more, God brings the 'more'. May we live in joyful expectation of the Spirit of God's 'more' and be open to receiving it and living it.

MS

The Word of love made flesh

The next day John again was standing with two of his disciples, and as he watched Jesus walk by, he exclaimed, 'Look, here is the Lamb of God!' The two disciples heard him say this, and they followed Jesus. When Jesus turned and saw them following, he said to them, 'What are you looking for?' They said to him, 'Rabbi' (which translated means Teacher), 'where are you staying?' He said to them, 'Come and see.' They came and saw where he was staying, and they remained with him that day. It was about four o'clock in the afternoon.

So far we have been contemplating some of God's words of love that have come to us via the wisdom handed down through the centuries and their intuitions of the untiring and uncompromising nature of his care for his children.

Now we move to a more immediate dimension of that love, interpreted through the life and deeds of Jesus. In Jesus, we see what love looks like—not only in words, but in actions; in ways of being fully and perfectly human, with the call to make these ways our own until we, too, begin to love with something of God's love. An e-mailed Christmas greeting puts it very well: 'Jesus is God's love with skin on it!'

Today, Jesus teaches us the first lesson in love: 'Come and see for yourselves. Don't just obey what I say, but do as I do. To find out what I do, how I live, you need to come and get to know me intim-ately. You need to come and abide with me and discover who I am and what I am all about.'

Children, as we know to our cost, learn from who we are and what we do much more than from what we tell them they ought to do. Today, Jesus invites us to embark on a journey of discovery, to come and see what God's love looks like with skin on it. It is a journey that will call us ever more deeply into the presence of God's eternal word of love.

Reflection

Jesus is inviting you today to 'come and see' in a particular way. Look back over the day's events and notice what it was that he wanted to show you of his love today.

MS

Seeing with the eyes of love

The next day Jesus decided to go to Galilee. He found Philip and said to him, 'Follow me.' Now Philip was from Bethsaida, the city of Andrew and Peter. Philip found Nathanael and said to him, 'We have found him about whom Moses in the law and also the prophets wrote, Jesus son of Joseph from Nazareth.' Nathanael said to him, 'Can anything good come out of Nazareth?' Philip said to him, 'Come and see.' When Jesus saw Nathanael coming towards him, he said of him, 'Here is truly an Israelite in whom there is no deceit!' Nathanael asked him, 'Where did you get to know me?' Jesus answered, 'I saw you under the fig tree before Philip called you.'

Yesterday we were invited to 'come and see'—to see for ourselves what God's love looks like in human form and discover for ourselves what that love will ask of us. Will we, though, see the reality or only what we expect to see?

Imagine a maternity ward in your local hospital. Imagine the rows of little cots there, each one containing what could be mistaken for a crumply little beetroot that screams loudly from time to time. A cynical observer might dismiss them as 'just babies and not very pretty at that', but now imagine the proud new parents beside their newborns. For them, those babies are the most beautiful beings God ever created. Who is seeing the reality? On the face of it, most newborns are, indeed, a bit crumply and red, but the eyes of those who love them will see reflected in those faces all the dreams that went into their making and all the hopes that will accompany them through their lives.

Nathanael provides a classic example of this difference in points of view. He 'sees' a man from Nazareth and immediately wraps him in his inherited prejudices about that place. Jesus, however, sees straight to the heart of Nathanael. It isn't some esoteric gift that Jesus has—he has simply seen Nathanael under the fig tree, like everyone else—but he has seen beyond the outward appearance to the real heart of the man. He has seen him with the eyes of God's love.

Reflection

Whatever masks we wear, whatever persona we construct for ourselves, the love of God sees the heart.

MS

Love that can be trusted

'Therefore I tell you, do not worry about your life, what you will eat or what you will drink, or about your body, what you will wear. Is not life more than food, and the body more than clothing? Look at the birds of the air; they neither sow nor reap nor gather into barns, and yet your heavenly Father feeds them. Are you not of more value than they? And can any of you by worrying add a single hour to your span of life? And why do you worry about clothing? Consider the lilies of the field, how they grow; they neither toil nor spin, yet I tell you, even Solomon in all his glory was not clothed like one of these. But if God so clothes the grass of the field, which is alive today and tomorrow is thrown into the oven, will he not much more clothe you?'

Has Jesus lost touch with reality here? Is it ever possible to live as free of anxiety as he suggests, especially in our fearladen 21st-century societies? So, are these just empty words? A parent whispers to a troubled child, 'Don't worry, everything will be all right, you'll see' while cradling the child close. A caring doctor reassures a frightened patient at the start of some new course of treatment, 'Don't worry now, trust me and you'll be fine.' Are these just empty words? The child's sorrows may not vanish overnight. The patient may not recover. Are the words of comfort and love then simply useless platitudes?

I am told that, when a person is drowning, the lifesaver can't actually help that person until and unless he or she stops struggling.

When the person finally gives up the fight and lets the lifesaver carry him or her, then the rescue can be undertaken.

Jesus doesn't offer us a quick fix for all our problems but, rather, a space in his heart that we can truly trust. As for the troubled child or the anxious patient or the drowning swimmer, the words 'Let go and trust in the one who can help you' are the key to new possibilities of healing and help.

Reflection

God doesn't say, 'What you fear will never happen', but, rather, 'What you fear may well happen, but you and I together can handle it.'

MS

Drawing from the source of love

Immediately [Jesus] made his disciples get into the boat and go on ahead to the other side, to Bethsaida, while he dismissed the crowd. After saying farewell to them, he went up on the mountain to pray. When evening came, the boat was out on the sea, and he was alone on the land. When he saw that they were straining at the oars against an adverse wind, he came towards them early in the morning, walking on the sea. He intended to pass them by. But when they saw him walking on the sea, they thought it was a ghost and cried out; for they all saw him and were terrified. But immediately he spoke to them and said, 'Take heart, it is I; do not be afraid.' Then he got into the boat with them and the wind ceased.

Today, again, Jesus' way of showing love seems strange—at least at first. He sends off his disciples to tackle the fickle currents of the Sea of Galilee when the wind is against them and the night is falling. He himself takes off to the mountains to pray. I have sometimes wondered how they would have reacted to this, as they struggled against the mounting turbulence on the waters, straining at the oars and desperately needing him to be with them. I guess most of us know in some way how that can feel, when we are struggling in hostile conditions and wondering where God has hidden himself.

Perhaps I can share with you how I was once praying with this passage and trying to imagine myself at the scene, including what I might have wanted to say to Jesus—something like, 'Why did you leave me alone like that when the wind was against me?' I still remember the 'answer' that seemed to suggest itself and has helped me so much in similar situations since then: 'But Margaret, I was with the Father, drawing on God's strength for both of us.'

Having drawn on the Father's strength and love, Jesus then comes to his friends in their hour of need. Thus strengthened, the impossible becomes possible and the storm abates.

Reflection

When desperation clouds our vision, God's love quietly does what we most deeply need.

MS

Turning love into action

Soon afterwards [Jesus] went to a town called Nain, and his disciples and a large crowd went with him. As he approached the gate of the town, a man who had died was being carried out. He was his mother's only son, and she was a widow; and with her was a large crowd from the town. When the Lord saw her, he had compassion for her and said to her, 'Do not weep.' Then he came forward and touched the bier, and the bearers stood still. And he said, 'Young man, I say to you, rise!' The dead man sat up and began to speak, and Jesus gave him to his mother.

Have you ever turned away from the TV screen and thought, 'I just can't take in the extent of the suffering in the world. How can I possibly begin to do anything about it?' Perhaps today's words of love can help us, by showing us how Jesus reacts.

First, he reacts to a specific situation of need. We are given the details. It happens in a town called Nain. It happens to a widow. She has lost her only son. This isn't about 'How can I solve the problem of poverty in the world?' but 'How am I going to respond to this particular point of need that I have encountered?'

Second, he responds with compassion. To feel compassion is to feel with the person who is suffering; to allow their pain to become also in some sense your own pain. The catalyst for Jesus' intervention is his compassion for this woman who has lost all she had.

Finally, there is the intervention itself. Jesus restores the young man to life and gives him back to the one who needs him. We can't do that—or can we? There are many ways to restore the spark of life to another person. Sometimes a smile alone is enough or a kind word in a phone call or a letter. Sometimes more engagement is demanded: the gift of food or time or comfort.

Whatever is asked of us, it begins with the particular situation, not the generalized need. It continues with compassion and it leads to action.

Reflection
We change the world only when we are willing to feel with the suffering that stands in front of us.

MS

Love is a decision

'But I say to you that listen, Love your enemies, do good to those who hate you, bless those who curse you, pray for those who abuse you. If anyone strikes you on the cheek, offer the other also; and from anyone who takes away your coat do not withhold even your shirt. Give to everyone who begs from you; and if anyone takes away your goods, do not ask for them again. Do to others as you would have them do to you. If you love those who love you, what credit is that to you? For even sinners love those who love them. If you do good to those who do good to you, what credit is that to you? For even sinners do the same. If you lend to those from whom you hope to receive, what credit is that to you? Even sinners lend to sinners, to receive as much again. But love your enemies, do good, and lend, expecting nothing in return.'

It has been wisely said, by M. Scott Peck in his book *The Road Less Travelled* (Hutchinson, 1983), that love is not an emotion; love is a decision. Unfortunately, we tend to regard 'love' as a matter of feeling. So Jesus' command to 'love our enemies' comes as a huge shock because, however hard we try, we are just not going to feel loving towards those who have harmed or abused us.

My friend Tina is caring for an elderly mother-in-law. The patient has been abusive towards Tina for as long as I have known them. She has never had a good word to say for her and never misses an opportunity to be unpleasant.

Tina has often been at the end of her tether and has admitted to feeling very angry and resentful towards her mother-in-law. She feels as though she has thoroughly failed the test of love. In fact, she has passed it with flying colours because she is doing exactly what Jesus is asking of us in today's reading. She is making a decision, every day, to do the more loving thing, in spite of the fact that all her feelings are straining against it and her only reward will be yet more abuse from her ungrateful patient.

Reflection

In what way might God be asking you to make a 'decision for love'?

MS

The prayer of love

'I ask not only on behalf of these, but also on behalf of those who will believe in me through their word, that they may all be one. As you, Father, are in me and I am in you, may they also be in us, so that the world may believe that you have sent me. The glory that you have given me I have given them, so that they may be one, as we are one, I in them and you in me, that they may become completely one, so that the world may know that you have sent me and have loved them even as you have loved me... Righteous Father, the world does not know you, but I know you; and these know that you have sent me. I made your name known to them, and I will make it known, so that the love with which you have loved me may be in them, and I in them.'

We have listened to some of God's words of love to his people in ancient times and we have watched as Jesus turns those words of love into practical action and invites us to do the same. Now Jesus comes to his own last days on earth and his words of love become a heartfelt prayer—not only for his first-century friends but also, explicitly, for us, his 21st-century friends.

Jesus prays that love might make us one, with each other and with God. To be completely united in our joy would be fantastic, of course, but what about being completely united in our pain and suffering? What if your suffering should also be mine? What if the suffering of the entire world were also to be mine? It's hard enough to be alongside a single beloved

person in their suffering. Imagine that 'oneness' multiplied across the whole of humanity, then you can begin to get a clue as to the extent and depth of God's love.

The oneness for which Jesus prays is costly beyond belief, yet it brings us to the very heart of God.

Reflection

Take a moment to be still today and let Jesus' prayer soak into your heart, perhaps substituting your own name for 'them'. These are his personal words of love to you.

MS

Becoming words of love

Beloved, let us love one another, because love is from God; everyone who loves is born of God and knows God. Whoever does not love does not know God, for God is love. God's love was revealed among us in this way: God sent his only Son into the world so that we might live through him. In this is love, not that we loved God but that he loved us and sent his Son to be the atoning sacrifice for our sins. Beloved, since God loved us so much, we also ought to love one another. No one has ever seen God; if we love one another, God lives in us, and his love is perfected in us. By this we know that we abide in him and he in us, because he has given us of his Spirit… God is love, and those who abide in love abide in God, and God abides in them.

In a memorable sermon, the minister invited us to imagine a stranger coming up to us in the street, looking for God and asking where he might find him. Where would you direct such a seeker yourself?

As I walked into my local town this morning I saw God's love everywhere. I overheard snippets of conversation: 'So good to see you. How are you feeling now?' 'Have you seen so-and-so? How did her operation go?' I saw drivers stop where they didn't need to stop, to let pedestrians cross the road. I noticed the patience and care in the eyes of a man pushing his wife along in a wheelchair. A friendly shop assistant took a lot of trouble to find what I wanted and the checkout girl beamed a lovely smile to those she served. A card came from a friend to say she was thinking about me in a difficult situation and a neighbour asked if I needed anything.

All these people, without even thinking about it, were choosing the more loving way of walking their daily paths. All were a challenge to me to do the same. Every one of them was a word of love from God's heart to mine.

Reflection

Every time we make a decision to do the more loving thing in a given situation, we are becoming words of love.

MS

1 Corinthians 9—12

Most organizations need leaders to function and, in the secular world, broadly speaking, there are three types. There are bad leaders who make decisions, boss everyone about and never lift a finger to help. There are good leaders who make decisions, encourage everyone and contribute their own gifts to the overall task. Then there are great leaders who take it a stage further by symbolizing, or 'modelling', the product. When that happens, they are emulated (imitated, even) by those within their organization, while those outside it often come to seek help.

The Church, like any other organization, needs leadership, but the difference is that, in the Church, it's not a pragmatic solution to an organizational need but a spiritual task. It isn't exercised (or shouldn't be!) by bossing others around or even by encouraging, but by modelling Christ. Paul, though, doesn't distinguish between 'leaders' and 'followers'. He expects every Christian to share the task of leadership in some form and expects God to gift everyone for ministry. His constant reminder to the Corinthian Christians is that they should model Christ. In other words, God calls every Christian to greatness.

In Corinth, secular culture kept derailing the church. The people's attitudes to worship, morality and leadership were all shaped by their secular values. Paul refers to these issues, but doesn't dwell on them. Instead, he wants the Corinthians to model Christ. He wants them to see themselves as God sees them, accept the gifts that God gives them and stop measuring themselves by the secular yardstick 'success'.

We may belong to a church that touches so many lives that it grows into a megachurch. We may be members of a congregation that develops a comprehensive range of activities for both church and community. We may be part of a church that is packed and funded by like-minded people. Equally, we may not. If not, it doesn't make our church 'less successful'. The yardstick used by God is obedience, not results.

Every Christian who models Christ and encourages others to do the same is a success because, when that happens, others emulate that person and begin to model Christ themselves. Any church, large or small, that models Christ is a success and those outside it will come to find out more.

David Robertson

1 CORINTHIANS 9:1–6 (NIV)

Professional leadership?

Am I not free? Am I not an apostle? Have I not seen Jesus our Lord? Are you not the result of my work in the Lord? Even though I may not be an apostle to others, surely I am to you! For you are the seal of my apostleship in the Lord. This is my defence to those who sit in judgment on me. Don't we have the right to food and drink? Don't we have the right to take a believing wife along with us, as do the other apostles and the Lord's brothers and Cephas? Or is it only I and Barnabas who must work for a living?

God calls everyone to serve the Church, but, here's a question: should some leaders be paid for it? Is modelling Christ a job? Different churches come to different conclusions on this issue, which seems to reflect New Testament practice. Evidently some apostles were 'paid' while others, such as Paul, were not.

It's easy to see why some apostles were paid. In order for Peter, for example, to be fully committed to prayer and proclamation, the church in Jerusalem would have to take care of not only his needs but also the needs of his wife (mentioned in today's passage) and, presumably, those of his family (see Acts 2:44–45; 6:2–4). By the time Paul wrote this letter, this wasn't just the norm, it was regarded as a command from the Lord (1 Corinthians 9:14).

Paul says that he had every right to be supported by the Church, but chose, instead, to support himself by working. Why? Surely a full-time Paul would have been more effective than a part-time Paul? It may have been because he thought that in consumer-orientated Corinth, financial support would be misunderstood. It would be interpreted as a 'transaction', and he feared that people would try to 'buy' the gospel. We don't know. What we do know is that he thought that receiving support would somehow hinder his modelling of Christ and he was determined to deflect the focus of his ministry away from himself and keep it firmly on his Lord and Saviour.

The question for us, of course, is this: whether we are leaders or members, paid or unpaid, can we say the same?

Prayer

Lord, help me to forgo any 'right' that gets in the way of modelling you.

DR

1 Corinthians 9:19–23 (NIV, abridged)

A voluntary slave

Though I am free and belong to no one, I make myself a slave to everyone, to win as many as possible... To those under the law I became like one under the law... so as to win those under the law. To those not having the law I became like one not having the law... so as to win those not having the law. To the weak I became weak, to win the weak. I have become all things to all people so that by all possible means I might save some. I do all this for the sake of the gospel, that I may share in its blessings.

We know quite a lot about Paul through the book of Acts and his letters. We know that he cited God as his authority and was prepared to argue with anyone—churches, other apostles, Jewish leaders and even Romans—so in what sense could he claim to be anyone's slave?

To appreciate this passage, we need to understand slavery as Paul knew it. Yes, slaves did as they were told, but, in that sense, Paul had only one master—Jesus—and he obeyed no one else. Slaves, though, became part of their master's household and identified with it; they accepted its customs and values and, in most cases, adopted its religion. It's this facet of slavery that Paul is referring to in today's passage: he became a cultural chameleon, blending in with all kinds of different attitudes, values and religious expressions in order to focus on the only thing that really mattered: modelling Christ.

In the 1980s, Meat Loaf had a hit with the song 'I'd do anything for love', the lyrics of which continued 'but I won't do that'. Paul is saying, 'I'd do anything for Christ—even that', which is an approach that challenges many of us. There are so many environments in which we, as Christians, may feel uncomfortable (the betting shop, biker pub, girlie binge night out and so forth) because we disapprove of the behaviour, values and consequences. Well, so did Paul—that's clear from his writing—but, instead of judging others, he joined them, modelled Christ and invited them to judge him. He thought that he would only be able to lead people to Christ if he was with them.

Prayer

Lord, I'd rather be nervously useful than serenely alone.

DR

The game of life

Do you not know that in a race all the runners run, but only one gets the prize? Run in such a way as to get the prize. Everyone who competes in the games goes into strict training. They do it to get a crown that will not last; but we do it to get a crown that will last for ever. Therefore I do not run like someone running aimlessly; I do not fight like someone beating the air. No, I beat my body and make it my slave so that after I have preached to others, I myself will not be disqualified for the prize.

Is it surprising that Paul does not take salvation for granted? Is the idea that he might be judged a 'goat' rather than a 'sheep' (Matthew 25:31–46) alarming? If so, we've confused Christian ministry with salvation. Paul hasn't and he knows that it's possible for him to lead others to Christ while he, himself, is actually far from the Lord.

Paul teaches that, when we preach, serve, minister and so forth, God provides gifts to help us accomplish these tasks. When we minister, we simply wield tools for the task, which says nothing about our spiritual health. It's possible to be a high-profile Christian leader who exercises a powerful ministry, while in our hidden, inner selves we may have drifted far, far away. The challenge here is that Paul says that, if he isn't careful, he could be like that and, by implication, so could we, because it's possible to minister to others when we're not right ourselves.

On the other hand, it isn't possible to model Christ when we are distant from him. We can 'do' Christianity as a task, but the façade has a habit of slipping and revealing our hypocrisy. We can only be Christian fully through the indwelling of the Holy Spirit, and that's the work of God. Without it, modelling Christ isn't possible and Paul knows that. He understands, as an apostle, he's a high-profile leader and that he uses the gifts God has given him to preach the gospel. It's a hugely demanding task, though, and, if he's to model Christ, he must keep close to him.

Prayer

Lord, help me to rest on only you, not on what I do for you.

DR

1 Corinthians 10:1–5 (NIV)

The way things were

For I do not want you to be ignorant of the fact, brothers and sisters, that our ancestors were all under the cloud and that they all passed through the sea. They were all baptized into Moses in the cloud and in the sea. They all ate the same spiritual food and drank the same spiritual drink; for they drank from the spiritual rock that accompanied them, and that rock was Christ. Nevertheless, God was not pleased with most of them; their bodies were scattered over the desert.

In Exodus, Moses led God's people out of Egypt and into the desert through the parted waters of the Red Sea—a kind of 'dry baptism' into their new life. As they lurched from crisis to crisis, God led them with a pillar of fire and cloud and provided manna for them to eat and water for them to drink. That period in the life of the nation of Israel became a symbol of their journey of faith and Paul here reinterprets that ancient journey as a symbol of Christian faith. He's using it as more than just a lesson about faith, though.

The exodus signified the fulfilment of the covenant between God and Abraham (Genesis 12:1–2). Released from Egypt, God's free people would dwell in their own land and be a blessing to the whole world. Paul wants the Corinthians to understand that, because of Christ, they are God's free people, the fulfilment of God's covenant, and a blessing to the world—and there's more.

The wilderness journey lasted for 40 years, but it didn't need to happen that way. There were opportunities to cross the Jordan, but no one who left Egypt ever did, not even Moses. That was left to Joshua and the next generation. Paul is suggesting that Christians can shy away from Christ's leading, that we can be God's people, but get 'stuck in the desert'—leaving it to the next generation to 'cross over' into whatever God was calling us to.

As we enter the season of Lent, a time when many impose on themselves some kind of 'desert regime', let's remember that God wants freedom and blessing for his people, not circularity and dryness. If Christ is to direct our daily walk, then our private faith will need to be matched by our public courage.

Prayer

*Lord, grant me the courage
to stay with you.*

DR

The way things are

Now these things occurred as examples to keep us from setting our hearts on evil things as they did. Do not be idolaters, as some of them were; as it is written: 'The people sat down to eat and drink and got up to indulge in pagan revelry.' We should not commit sexual immorality, as some of them did—and in one day twenty-three thousand of them died. We should not test the Lord, as some of them did—and were killed by snakes. And do not grumble, as some of them did—and were killed by the destroying angel.

Paul uses this difficult, shocking passage because he wants the Corinthians to contrast their past lives without Christ with the grace of God they now know. They have been forgiven because Jesus died on the cross, taking on himself the consequences of their sin. Jesus does not change (Hebrews 13:8), but neither does sin—even if Corinthian culture says otherwise.

Let's test our own culture. In today's passage Paul mentions idolatry. Most of us will agree that it's wrong to worship false gods and we don't do it. No cultural change there, then. Mind you, what is celebrity culture if not idolatry? Is our society really that different from that of first-century Corinth? What about sexual immorality—how does our culture compare there?

'Oh, but…', we say, 'that's secular culture, not Christian culture. Christians live counter-culturally!' That's a relief, then. How wonderful that in our churches there's no idolatry, no sexual immorality… and no grumbling?

Is it a surprise to see grumbling mentioned in the same breath as sexual immorality? If it is, then our values have been changed by our culture and don't reflect the unchangeable Christ, because grumbling has its root in original sin. When we grumble, we expect everyone else (and maybe even God) to change in order to suit our needs. It indicates selfishness and pride and it's the opposite of repentance, humility and a readiness to come to the cross of Christ.

According to Paul, grumbling is an example of how easily God's people can forget God's values. In our own walk with the unchangeable Christ, it's a reminder that we, too, can so easily trip up.

Prayer

Lord, grant me strength to live a truly counter-cultural life.

DR

1 Corinthians 10:12–13, 16–17 (NIV)

One in Christ

So, if you think you are standing firm, be careful that you don't fall! No temptation has seized you except what is common among people. And God is faithful; he will not let you be tempted beyond what you can bear. But when you are tempted, he will also provide a way out so that you can stand up under it... Is not the cup of thanksgiving for which we give thanks a participation in the blood of Christ? And is not the bread that we break a participation in the body of Christ? Because there is one loaf, we, who are many, are one body, for we all partake of the one loaf.

There are two issues in this passage. The first is pride, which is a 'deadly sin' because it reveals that we think we know better than God, we can live our lives without him, thank you very much. When we come to Christ, we admit our pride, seek forgiveness and entrust our lives to him. As we become used to living for Christ, though, we can become blasé about the strength of Christ within us and come to believe that it's *our* strength. When that happens, it's the same old pride and independence emerging in a new guise.

The second issue is temptation. Before we meet Christ, we may just give in to it (especially if we are culturally conditioned to think that there's nothing wrong with our behaviour). When we meet Christ, however, we begin to see our cultural values through his unchanging eyes and then struggle with temptation. Do we think,

though, that one day we shall be so mature, so strong in Christ, that we shall never have any more problems with temptation? That's pride again.

If we think that temptation is a private, inner struggle, then it will overcome us. Unless we trust 'the way out' that God has provided, we shall lose every battle. God's 'way out' is Jesus. Remember the playground bully? Temptation is that bully and, when we are tempted, we need to fetch our 'big brother' to fight for us. If we try to resist alone, we shall fail, so we admit our weakness, cry to Jesus and stand in his shadow while he defeats the bully.

Prayer

Lord, I am weak. I trust in your strength.

DR

Living where we live

If some unbeliever invites you to a meal and you want to go, eat whatever is put before you without raising questions of conscience. But if anyone says to you, 'This has been offered in sacrifice,' then do not eat it, both for the sake of the one who told you and for conscience' sake... Do not cause anyone to stumble, whether Jews, Greeks or the church of God—even as I try to please everybody in every way. For I am not seeking my own good but the good of many, so that they may be saved.

Every culture tends to veer towards certain moral problems. From Paul's letters, we can see that the Corinthians tended to lean towards materialism, idolatry and sexual immorality. Living a righteous Christian life in such a culture was hard and they, like Paul, really tried to 'please everybody in every way'. Wouldn't that involve a compromise of principles? Well, yes and no.

Paul was brought up as a Pharisee (Philippians 3:5), which meant that he was taught to be fastidious about ritual cleanliness. Yet here he is advocating a 'don't ask' policy about meat (offered to idols before being sold in the market). To compromise such an ingrained principle must have been hard for Paul and others like him. Equally, however, he says that if the host declares the meat 'idol fodder', then the right thing to do is refuse it.

His concern is not the meat itself (or the idols), but the people. He is saying, in effect, 'Be ready to compromise your cultural principles, but never compromise on Christ. Make clear to those who have not yet heard about Christ that you don't regard yourselves as superior in any sense. At the same time, try to make sure that those who already trust Christ won't be so offended by your actions that they lose sight of their Saviour.'

It's a difficult balance to get right—for Paul, the Corinthian Christians and us. Yet, it's the balance that we must achieve because Jesus did and still does. If we are to follow him into our culture, we shall need to learn where to compromise and what, or rather who, to hold on to.

Prayer

Lord, teach me to trust you when I'm out of my depth.

DR

Conflicting cultures

Now I want you to realize that the head of every man is Christ, and the head of the woman is man, and the head of Christ is God... For man did not come from woman, but woman from man; neither was man created for woman, but woman for man... In the Lord, however, woman is not independent of man, nor is man independent of woman. For as woman came from man, so also man is born of woman. But everything comes from God.

The early Church was made up of a variety of cultures. Some people, and all of the apostles, were Jewish. Others, such as the Corinthians, had a Greek background and still others were Roman. One example of this cultural diversity was their differing attitudes to male headship.

In Jewish culture, the man of the house learned the Law and then not only taught it but also embodied it to his wife, children and servants. That would have been the model Paul grew up with. In Greek households, however, women could hold authority, too (as Lydia did in Acts 16:15). So, if Christians were seeking to model Christ, which was the correct model for the Church? Should the Greek Christians be counter-cultural and proclaim male headship or should the Jewish Christians be counter-cultural and proclaim interchangeability?

In Corinth, and elsewhere, Christians were wrestling with this issue and, in his letter, Paul takes a 'both/and' approach. He stands by his Jewish principles that women should be dependent on their husbands, but recognizes that men should also be dependent on their wives! In another of his letters, he states clearly that gender is neither here nor there (Galatians 3:28).

The issue of 'male headship' is still current in the Church. We don't have room to unpack the issues here, but may simply see it as an example of the challenges thrown up by conflicting cultures. If we only ever seek to share Christ with like-minded people, then our own attitudes will never be challenged and we may well assume that what we think is correct. If instead we share Christ with people whose values are different from our own, sooner or later we shall have to examine issues we may never have considered before.

Reflection

Are there cultural assumptions in my church that should be questioned?

DR

Culture in the church

Every man who prays or prophesies with his head covered dishonours his head. And every woman who prays or prophesies with her head uncovered dishonours her head—it is just as though her head were shaved. If a woman does not cover her head, she should have her hair cut off; and if it is a disgrace for a woman to have her hair cut or shaved off, she should cover her head.

In one sense, this is another facet of the male/female headship issue. In Jewish culture, women could not pray or prophesy in a 'congregation'. They could do so if they wanted to in the temple courtyard but, during temple worship or in the synagogue, they were separated from the men and did not contribute. Here, however, Paul suggests ways in which women might properly exercise public ministries so that the Church would be neither exactly Jewish nor Greek in its culture, but have a whole new culture of its own.

The focus here is on headgear (similar to that still worn by women in the Near East) and the issue is one of freedom in Christ. These are Christian women and, now that Jesus is their Lord, they wonder whether they still have to obey the cultural norms of Corinth. In this instance, Paul says, 'Yes', because the only women who went about bareheaded were the prostitutes! So, if church women exercise their 'freedom in Christ' by discarding their cultural headgear, the message they are sending to visitors to the church is, 'Welcome to the brothel' —not an appropriate message to give!

In our own culture, there may be fashions in dress or speech that should not be adopted by Christians. Yes, we have freedom in Christ and these things, like meat offered to idols, cannot harm us, but what about those who are seeking Christ? When they see us, what will they think? There's a fine line between accepting cultural compromise in order to be 'all things to all people' and embracing inappropriate cultural mores. There is a line, though, and, if we are to keep on Christ's side of it, our motives will show the truth. To compromise for Christ is evangelism; to assert our freedom regardless of the consequences is pride.

Prayer

Lord, because I am free I choose to submit my life to you.

DR

One Church

When you come together, it is not the Lord's Supper you eat, for as you eat, each of you goes ahead without waiting for anybody else. One remains hungry, another gets drunk… Therefore, whoever eats the bread or drinks the cup of the Lord in an unworthy manner will be guilty of sinning against the body and blood of the Lord. We ought to examine ourselves before we eat of the bread and drink of the cup. For those who eat and drink without recognizing the body of the Lord eat and drink judgment on themselves.

To us, familiar as we are with formal worship, this description of the Corinthian version of breaking bread can beggar belief. What were these Christians doing—gorging and drinking while others stood by hungry?

The answer is simple: they were organizing their worship after the fashion of their pre-Christian lives. Had they been Jewish, they would have been brought up with father-led family worship at home, regular trips to the synagogue for teaching and occasional visits to the temple to make sacrifices. They weren't Jewish converts, however, but Corinthians, and much of their pre-Christian worship would have entailed an excess of food, drink and even sex. What they were doing now was what they'd always done when worshipping their old gods— and maybe they even thought that they were being restrained!

Paul tackles this issue by directing them to Christ. He doesn't berate the Corinthians for bringing their old ways into the new patterns of worship, but just points out that they are making their communion with Jesus. In other words, their focus should be on Christ's grace and forgiveness and their own unworthiness. It's an approach Paul often takes: instead of highlighting an issue in a way that makes it seem even bigger, he directs people to Jesus because behaviour is only ever a symptom and he trusts his Lord, and theirs, to sort them out.

When a difference of opinion arises in our churches, how do we tackle the issue? Ignore it and hope it'll go away? Whip up support on both sides? Try to come to a reasonable compromise? Turn to Jesus, focus on him and expect him to sort it out—not the argument, but us?

Reflection

When the Lord sees our worship, what does he see?

DR

73

Spiritual life

Now about spiritual gifts, brothers and sisters, I do not want you to be ignorant. You know that when you were pagans, somehow or other you were influenced and led astray to mute idols. Therefore I tell you that no one who is speaking by the Spirit of God says, 'Jesus be cursed', and no one can say, 'Jesus is Lord', except by the Holy Spirit. There are different kinds of gifts, but the same Spirit. There are different kinds of service, but the same Lord. There are different kinds of working, but the same God works all of them in everyone.

In Paul's teaching, spiritual gifts are 'God-given abilities' and distinct from 'natural talents'. In the verses that follow, which we shall look at tomorrow, he mentions speaking in tongues, working miracles and prophecy as being among these gifts rather than 'natural talents', such as musical ability. Spiritual gifts are, by definition, 'spiritual' in origin and it is therefore necessary to discern just which 'spirit' is stimulating them.

That was an issue in Corinth and Paul directs the church to Jesus, saying, in effect, 'Don't focus on how people go about their ministry or on who is exercising which ministry. Look, instead, at the results. Ask, "Is Jesus being exalted and glorified?" If he is, the gifts are godly and the ministry should be encouraged. If not, they're not, and the ministry should be stopped.'

In our churches, we often want to know in detail what is being proposed before we give permission it to begin. We can also be conservative about who exercises their gifts. The upside of this approach is that it emphasizes safety and responsibility. The downside is that it can easily suffocate godly initiatives and gifted, but inconsistent, people. Paul seems to have approached ministry from the opposite direction, expecting everyone to exercise their gifts and then discern which ministries were godly and which were not. The upside of his approach was that there was freedom. The downside was that there was freedom, which, in Corinth, led to all kinds of problems.

Godly leaders such Paul, however, prefer freedom, even when it leads to mistakes, because it encourages Christians to depend on God and grow to spiritual maturity.

Prayer

Lord, help me to offer ministry humbly but courageously.

DR

The Spirit of God

Now to each one the manifestation of the Spirit is given for the common good. To one there is given through the Spirit the message of wisdom, to another the message of knowledge by means of the same Spirit, to another faith by the same Spirit, to another gifts of healing by that one Spirit, to another miraculous powers, to another prophecy, to another distinguishing between spirits, to another speaking in different kinds of tongues, and to still another the interpretation of tongues. All these are the work of one and the same Spirit, and he gives them to each one, just as he determines.

Paul is an apostle, evangelist, church planter and leader, but he doesn't expect to exercise ministry alone, doing everything himself. He expects the Holy Spirit to distribute different gifts to different people and for ministry to be shared. He expects everyone to do something (a style of ministry we now call 'collaborative').

Many churches today struggle with this approach. After all, if we trust everyone with ministry (especially with highly visible, 'upfront' ministry), won't some people cause all kinds of problems? Without a clear hierarchy to keep a tight grip on things, won't we end up with chaos? To be fair, the answer to both questions may be 'Yes'. Look at Corinth: it was a church planted by Paul and led by Paul along collaborative lines and look at the mess and anarchy there was there!

In spite of this, Paul doesn't issue orders; nor does he expect Corinthian 'ministers' to flex their leadership muscles and sort things out. Why not? Because the church didn't function that way. Ministry belonged to everyone according to their gifting as determined by God. The only 'leader' Paul consistently refers to is Jesus.

That last point is the heart of it. It's quite possible for a well-organized, talented group of Christians to get on with 'being a church' and leave Jesus out entirely. When Jesus is in charge, though, he has a habit of calling the most unlikely people to surprising ministries (such as Paul) and giving gifts even to those who get things wrong (such as the Corinthians).

Prayer

Lord, thank you that ministry is not about what I can do for you, but what you can do with and through me.

DR

The spiritual body

The body is a unit, though it is made up of many parts; and though all its parts are many, they form one body. So it is with Christ. For we were all baptized by one Spirit into one body—whether Jews or Greeks, slave or free—and we were all given the one Spirit to drink... If the whole body were an eye, where would the sense of hearing be? If the whole body were an ear, where would the sense of smell be? But in fact God has arranged the parts in the body, every one of them, just as he wanted them to be. If they were all one part, where would the body be? As it is, there are many parts, but one body.

The Corinthians evidently hankered after personal glory. As is still sometimes the case in Christian circles, it was disguised as a desire for the 'high-profile' ministries, such as teaching. A basic principle of such ministry is that the 'glory' must be deflected away from the minister and on to Jesus. Indeed, the desire to be an 'upfront minister' can, in itself, be a sign that there's a problem. Those who desire such ministry would do well to read James 3:1.

Paul tackles this issue by using the image of the body. Every part is vital so it doesn't matter what our ministry is. What does matter is that we are obedient to the call and gifting of God. The body has only one head—Jesus Christ—and he should be the only one in the Church who has a high profile. It's up to him how he equips the rest of us. As Paul says, if the Church

was organized by us, we'd probably focus on some ministries and forget about others. If that happened, Christ's body would be just a big eye or a huge ear—in other words, monstrous!

It's good to remember that every Christian is vital to the worldwide body of Christ, whether we live in the UK or in Papua New Guinea (the focus of today's Women's World Day of Prayer). We are all loved by Jesus, all given gifts for ministry and, as we each play our prayerful part, look at what Jesus does with the whole!

Prayer

*Lord, you love us, join us together
and gift us. Thank you.*

DR

1 CORINTHIANS 12:27–31 (NIV)

One in Christ

Now you are the body of Christ, and each one of you is a part of it. And in the church God has appointed first of all apostles, second prophets, third teachers, then workers of miracles, also those having gifts of healing, those able to help others, those with gifts of administration, and those speaking in different kinds of tongues. Are all apostles? Are all prophets? Are all teachers? Do all work miracles? Do all have gifts of healing? Do all speak in tongues? Do all interpret? But eagerly desire the greater gifts.

If we work really hard, we can construct a hierarchical leadership structure from this passage. It requires only one apostle, a couple of prophets, a few more teachers and so forth. It also needs a substantial congregation who do nothing but congregate in order to receive from these ministers. Here, though (and elsewhere), Paul is not talking about a few leaders—he's talking about everyone in the church. So, if everyone was exercising one of these ministries, what would the church look like?

It would look like a big, complex country dance—the sort where people dance in one place, change partners and dance again in a new position. Church members would exercise ministry and leadership where appropriate, but elsewhere accept the ministry and leadership of others. They would be, by turns, leaders and followers, encouragers and encouraged, ministering and ministered to.

In that church, no one person would model Christ for the benefit of everyone else. Instead, everyone would seek to model Christ. No individual would be regarded as the high-profile leader: at various times, many different people would fulfil that role.

Of course, if Jesus had died on the cross and his life had finished there, the church could never be like that. If Jesus had risen, ascended and left us, the same would apply. It is only because Jesus sent his Spirit, his living presence, that it's possible for the church to collaborate in such a way. If his Spirit is among us, then he is the head of his body, ready to lead us and give gifts for ministry. As Paul says, again and again, it all comes down to Jesus.

Reflection

Any church, large or small, that models Christ is a success.

DR

Jesus on the road: Mark 1—2

The beginning of Mark's Gospel throws us in at the deep end. He focuses on what matters most to him—the fact that Jesus is the Son of God—and cuts out all surplus detail. He sets out his main themes at the start, which the other 15 chapters flesh out. His focus is so concentrated and his words so loaded with meaning that we can easily miss what is going on as they speed by.

Mark's approach is not so much to relate episodes in the life of Jesus as to introduce his big themes. Of course, it's important for him to get the facts right, but it matters even more why these things happened and what they can mean—for both Mark's first audience of early Christians and us now. So Mark presents us with 'cameos of doctrine… epitomising the message of the Gospel' (as the Revd Professor Leslie Houlden calls them in *The Common Worship Lectionary: A scripture commentary*, SPCK, 2002). Only near the end of these first two chapters does he get into the swing of the stories of Jesus' ministry. He is more interested in the ideas behind the events. For example, John the Baptist comes and goes very quickly at this point as, once he has played his part, the story moves on relentlessly.

All through his Gospel, Mark lets his readers in on what is seen as a secret: that Jesus, this ordinary-seeming man, is so much more than a remarkable teacher. Mark realizes that we might not guess from the stories of a travelling preacher, who died as a shamed criminal, that he is the beloved Son of God himself, the creator of the universe. No wonder those around him fail to recognize him. The disciples misunderstand him; the religious and secular authorities are suspicious of his charisma. Mark writes his Gospel partly to say that such people have missed the point. God came down to humankind and they didn't realize who he was.

Mark begins his Gospel not with the Christmas story, but with Jesus' universal significance as the Son of God. He continues by introducing John the Baptist and emphasizing that Jesus' authority comes from God. He gathers disciples and performs a number of healings, which bring him into conflict with the religious establishment. Mark is setting the scene for the ultimate battle—that between the loving God and the sinfulness of all our hearts.

Rachel Boulding

MARK 1:1–4, 7–8 (KJV, ABRIDGED)

The cosmic power of the Son of God

The beginning of the gospel of Jesus Christ, the Son of God; As it is written in the prophets, Behold, I send my messenger before thy face... The voice of one crying in the wilderness, Prepare ye the way of the Lord, make his paths straight. John did baptize in the wilderness, and preach the baptism of repentance for the remission of sins... saying... I indeed have baptized you with water: but he shall baptize you with the Holy Ghost.

Mark's startling opening plunges us right into his message. He tells us immediately the essence of his whole book: the fact that Jesus is the Son of God. As we shall see in these two chapters, Mark focused intensely on what his hearers and readers needed to know. They required this as a matter of life and death, so there was no need to distract them with less important information.

There are no stories of angels, a baby and a manger: this man Jesus is crucial only because he is the Son of God. The first verses set us in a cosmic plane, in which the prophets foretold the coming messenger. Then the idea is tied down specifically to an individual—John the Baptist. John is a dramatic figure: 'Parched body, hollow eyes, some uncouth thing Made him appear, long since from Earth exiled' (as the 17th-century poet William Drummond of Hawthornden put it). Yet Mark isn't really interested in him. He doesn't report much of what John actually preached—his message of repentance—but focuses on what he said about Jesus. What is vital is Jesus' extraordinary relationship with God.

As I suggested in the introduction, this was the most important fact about Jesus for Mark, yet the people around him missed it. We have no such excuse for not realizing who Jesus is, but, so often, we behave as if he were just another helpful person with some tips about life. We don't really accept his authority over every part of our lives. His rule is loving, but we don't trust his perfect love that casts out all fear.

Reflection

In what ways do I fail to recognize Jesus as the unique Son of God? Do I trust him fully with my time, money, decisions?

RB

Am I truly driven by the Spirit?

And it came to pass in those days, that Jesus came from Nazareth of Galilee, and was baptized of John in Jordan. And straightway coming up out of the water, he saw the heavens opened, and the Spirit like a dove descending upon him: And there came a voice from heaven, saying, Thou art my beloved Son, in whom I am well pleased. And immediately the Spirit driveth him into the wilderness. And he was there in the wilderness forty days, tempted of Satan; and was with the wild beasts; and the angels ministered unto him.

Again, we see how concise Mark is. The message is urgent. Matthew and Luke describe both Jesus' baptism and his temptation at greater length, with telling details of the nature of the temptations, but Mark focuses on the global significance of these things, emphasizing the fact that Jesus is loved and approved by God his Father and then that he was tested.

Some commentators have even seen the reference to the wild beasts as linking Jesus to Adam: he is the second Adam, making the wilderness a new Eden, where the animals are friendly. The testing demonstrates that Jesus beat Satan—a fact that became significant as he went about his ministry. He was about to do battle with unclean spirits and other forces of evil, so it is important that he had already won that victory.

The wilderness is, of course, a suitable subject for this season of the Church's year, which is why this passage was used in many churches just over a week ago, on the first Sunday of Lent. For many of us, it is a time of extra reading or study groups, but, as Professor Raymond Chapman writes in *Following the Gospel through the Year* (Canterbury Press, 2001), sometimes we need to remind ourselves of the basics that Mark stresses about Jesus, of his being driven to the wilderness *by the Spirit* (v. 12) and waited on there by angels (v. 13).

Reflection

'Lent always brings temptations, weariness in devotion, even resentment about what we have voluntarily undertaken in love. It also brings many blessings, spiritual growth, guidance of the kind traditionally associated with the angels, the messengers of God. As we begin, are we going in the confidence of our own strength, or are we truly driven by the Spirit?'

Raymond Chapman
RB

Having unique adventures on the way

Jesus came into Galilee, preaching the gospel of the kingdom of God, And saying, The time is fulfilled, and the kingdom of God is at hand: repent ye, and believe the gospel. Now as he walked by the sea of Galilee, he saw Simon and Andrew his brother casting a net into the sea: for they were fishers. And Jesus said unto them, Come ye after me, and I will make you to become fishers of men. And straightway they forsook their nets, and followed him.

Mark has outlined what his Gospel is all about and set out the main characters and why they matter. The rest of his work fills in the details, explaining what it all means.

Mark summarizes Jesus' teaching (v. 15), but without really saying what it consists of. We might well ask just what this gospel and this kingdom are really about, but it was enough for the disciples, who immediately abandoned their workplaces and followed him. The word that is translated 'straightway' or 'immediately' (*euthus*) crops up constantly in this Gospel. In repeating it, and in using his urgent, cut-to-the-chase style, Mark shows how pressing the message is. We need to do something now. Tomorrow won't do: we might think we'll be less busy, but the chance may have gone by then.

The disciples' instant response can be inspiring in 'its purity and positivity' (Leslie Houlden, *The Common Worship Lectionary: A scripture commentary*). It is the shining ideal that we should all follow. It can also, of course, be dispiriting: how can we possibly live up to it? We can't abandon our responsibilities. Perhaps we should remember that this was the glittering start to the disciples' careers of betrayal, persecution and (for most of them) execution. They might have begun well, but the rest of the Gospel depicts their bickering and misunderstandings of Jesus. They were sinners and learners (the latter being the meaning of 'disciples') just like us.

Reflection

*Try to recall the hopes
that brought you to Jesus.
He is the Way.
Follow Him through the
Land of Unlikeness;
You will see rare beasts,
and have unique adventures.*

'For the Time Being',
W.H. Auden (1907–73)

RB

Find the real source of authority

And they went into Capernaum; and straightway on the sabbath day he entered into the synagogue, and taught. And they were aston-ished at his doctrine: for he taught them as one that had authority, and not as the scribes. And there was in their synagogue a man with an unclean spirit; and he cried out, Saying, Let us alone; what have we to do with thee, thou Jesus of Nazareth? art thou come to destroy us? I know thee who thou art, the Holy One of God. And Jesus rebuked him, saying, Hold thy peace, and come out of him.

Now we are getting down to the business of actually bringing about the good news, as Jesus begins his ministry of healing. As usual with Mark, the style is concise. We don't hear anything about the sick man himself, just about the unclean spirit. Also, as happens elsewhere in the Gospel, it's not the event itself—the healing—that really matters, but what it says about who Jesus is and his mes-sage concerning the kingdom.

So, Mark reports that the un-clean spirit correctly identified Jesus. The witnesses to the healing and the religious authorities both failed to do this, which is odd as these two groups ought to be just the people to recognize Jesus as the Son of God. Today, too, it is sometimes the most unexpected people who realize what Jesus has to offer.

This also suggests why Jesus silenced the unclean spirit here and, later in the chapter and in the Gospels in general, he discouraged an emphasis on miracles. He per-forms them out of compassion (though the mention of his 'com-passion' to a leper later in this chapter is not often repeated) and to demonstrate the power of God, his Father, but he can do them only as part of the wider background of faith in the kingdom of God. What counts is not the miracles them-selves, but what the action says about Jesus and his divine power. For Jesus 'had authority' (v. 22). His authority was more than human credibility or skill in speak-ing; his power came from the Creator of the universe.

Reflection

Books, magazines, experts, counsel-lors and advisers all offer useful tips about life, but think about this question. What difference does it make to me today that Jesus 'had authority' and divine wisdom?

RB

How to bring someone to Jesus

Then some people came, bringing to him a paralysed man, carried by four of them. And when they could not bring him to Jesus because of the crowd, they removed the roof above him; and after having dug through it, they let down the mat on which the paralytic lay. When Jesus saw their faith, he said to the paralytic, 'Son, your sins are forgiven.' Now some of the scribes were sitting there, questioning in their hearts, '… It is blasphemy! Who can forgive sins but God alone?' At once Jesus… said to them, '… Which is easier, to say to the paralytic, "Your sins are forgiven", or to say, "Stand up and take your mat and walk"?'

Suddenly, Mark goes into detail. This is a proper story, with some neatly drawn characters, intriguing action and even a disagreement. It's a well-known episode because it's so vividly depicted: we can imagine the slightly comic scene of the crowds and the flat roof being dug through. We can feel involved. It is the friends bringing the paralysed man who are confident in Jesus' power to help: it is 'their faith' that Jesus sees (v. 5).

This has become a model for all our acts of trusting Jesus with those around us. We can bring our friends to him—whether in our prayers for them or in recommending him to them in what we do and say. If the friends hadn't bothered, the man wouldn't have been healed.

Then, the story picks up the themes from the previous chapter, in seeing what happens as being essentially bound up with Jesus' authority as the Son of God. Jesus, carefully separating forgiveness from healing, demonstrates that he has the power to do both—not in his own strength, though, but in God's. He says 'your sins are forgiven', implying 'by God', so pronouncing God's forgiveness, not his. Jesus presents the man to God for God to do the work of healing.

Sometimes we can make every effort—going to bizarre lengths such as cutting holes in roofs—but, in the end, we have to leave it to God. We can carry on praying for seemingly hopeless people and sometimes God can bring good out of the situation.

Reflection

What can I do in the next 24 hours that might suggest the love of God to someone?

RB

God forgive us all

When the scribes and the Pharisees saw that he [Jesus] was eating with sinners and tax collectors, they said to his disciples, 'Why does he eat with tax collectors and sinners?' When Jesus heard this, he said to them, 'Those who are well have no need of a physician, but those who are sick; I have come to call not the righteous but sinners.'

Mark now develops another of his themes: Jesus' disagreements with the religious authorities. As happens today in religious circles (as well as in others), the innovator is seen as a troublemaker, upsetting the safe little ways we tend to have. Jesus, teaching much that was in line with the good Judaism of his day, is questioned by the very people who ought to have welcomed him.

Many scholars emphasize Jesus' Jewishness and the links between his teachings and those of the rabbis and the Pharisees. Passages such as the Sermon on the Mount (Matthew 5—7) have even been described as 'pure Judaism'. Seen in this light, part of the scribes' and Pharisees' objection to Jesus is that they feel let down by one of their own. He could be a promising Jewish teacher, so it irritates them even more when he criticizes them for failing to live up to their own ideals.

With his talk of needing a physician, Jesus implies that the religious authorities are sinners, too. Those who think they are righteous are merely showing that they aren't righteous at all. Everyone needs God's forgiveness. Perhaps we shouldn't read it so much as a commentary on the specific religious groups of that time, but more—and more importantly for us now—as a searing analysis of the potential pitfalls of having a faith. Jesus speaks directly of the traps that each one of us can fall into easily, then and today. So, we all need to look into our hearts to check for any spiritual pride, smugness and condescension towards non-Christians.

Reflection

In Shakespeare's Macbeth, *the doctor who witnesses Lady Macbeth sleepwalking and confessing to murder observes, 'More needs she the divine than the physician—God, God forgive us all!' I have seen this played compassionately, putting her lurid sin into the context of us all being sinners in need of forgiveness.*

RB

The Lord of every bit of my life

One Sabbath he [Jesus] was going through the cornfields; and as they made their way his disciples began to pluck heads of grain. The Pharisees said to him, 'Look, why are they doing what is not lawful on the sabbath?' And he said to them, 'Have you never read what David did when he and his companions were hungry...? He... ate the bread of the Presence, which it is not lawful for any but the priests to eat, and he gave some to his companions.' Then he said to them, 'The sabbath was made for humankind, and not humankind for the sabbath; so the Son of Man is lord even of the sabbath.'

As we saw yesterday, it's far too easy to point to others' careful religious observances and think them fussy, while we, of course, see the bigger picture from our lofty heights. I have even read a book, written by a church leader, that used this very passage to argue we shouldn't bother to fight sin too much as it is inevitably in our nature. We always seem to need to be reminded that rules are there for a purpose and to provide a structure within which we can flourish.

The last sentence here is very radical and could be read as pointing towards sweeping away all laws, along the lines of the church leader's book. However, Jesus seems to suggest that we shouldn't dwell on the religious constructions of our own making but, instead, probe our real motivation. Are we going about things in a way that truly reflects God's love for each one of us and (as we saw yesterday) the fact that we've no right to think of ourselves as being better than the next person?

The sabbath is God's day of rest, set aside for us to refresh ourselves by both pausing from the daily grind and devoting ourselves to God. If Jesus is Lord even of the sabbath, in this wider sense, then he is the Lord of every part of our lives. We know that we should dedicate our work to him, but he is also the Lord of our time off, which becomes our re-creation. He fulfils our deepest wants—for work, rest, fun and love.

Reflection

Jesus is 'the living bread, in whom all our hungers are satisfied' (Common Worship, *Holy Communion* service).

RB

Zechariah: your kingdom come

Near the end of the Old Testament, we find what we often call 'the minor prophets'. It is not a very complimentary description and certainly not indicative of the treasures that they contain, but the poetic language that these prophets use and the strange visions they record can make their message difficult for us to unscramble. Here and there we find a verse that resonates with us or a passage throwing some new light on the person of Jesus Christ. For the most part, though, we may feel as if we are walking in a fog, hoping for some recognizable features.

If that is how you feel as you approach these readings from Zechariah, then take courage! The same Holy Spirit who inspired him is available to you and, as you plunge into this ocean of Hebrew poetry, visions and apocalyptic prophecy, you can be upheld by him and find yourself at the end of the next two weeks on the far shore, inspired and encouraged by Zechariah's message.

Zechariah lived around 500 years before the birth of Jesus and was called to prophesy to the people of God as they came to the end of their time of exile in Babylon and returned to Jerusalem to re-establish and rebuild it. Like his contemporary, Haggai, Zechariah's desire was to encourage the returning exiles. His message contains a glorious mixture of words of encouragement for the people around him, glimpses of the longed-for Messiah and what he would achieve and promises and warnings about the end of time and God's ultimate purposes for the world.

Those three elements seem to exist in all true prophecy. What is God saying to me, to my church, to my country today? What is God saying about Jesus Christ, his living word? What is God saying about my future and the future of the world? Look for these three elements as you work through the book of Zechariah. Perhaps take a notebook and jot down each day the message that you hear through his words.

Rather conveniently, there are 14 chapters in Zechariah, so we shall look at a chapter each day for the next 14 days. There is not room here to include the Bible text in full, so some key verses have been picked out, but do try to make time and read the whole chapter each day—you will find it more than worthwhile.

Jennifer Oldroyd

ZECHARIAH 1:1–4 (NRSV, ABRIDGED)

Return to me

In the eighth month, in the second year of Darius, the word of the Lord came to the prophet Zechariah son of Berechiah son of Iddo, saying: The Lord was very angry with your ancestors. Therefore say to them, Thus says the Lord of hosts: Return to me, says the Lord of hosts, and I will return to you, says the Lord of hosts. Do not be like your ancestors... [who] did not hear or heed me, says the Lord.

The exiles returning from Babylon to Jerusalem would have rejoiced at the end of their captivity and felt excitement at finally returning to the country and city of their destiny. However, they would also be bringing with them the same tendency to sin and disobedience that had resulted in their being exiled in the first place.

Zechariah was a relatively young man at this point and he had been appointed by God, along with his contemporary, Haggai, to encourage the returning exiles and ensure that they got their priorities right. Haggai concentrated on the absolute priority—rebuilding the temple. No matter that it wasn't as grand and beautiful as the previous building, it would only be by giving their time and energy to its construction that they would enjoy the blessing of God on their new life (Haggai 1:7–11).

Zechariah's parallel ministry pointed beyond the 'now' of the rebuilding and the resettling of the exiles towards a brighter future. He saw visions depicting the mercy of God and his anger with the nations that had taken the punishment of Israel beyond that which he had intended. He brought prophetic words to the returned exiles of God's comfort, blessing and prosperity and was shown glimpses of the coming Messiah and the new age that he was to bring.

Like Haggai, however, Zechariah knew that comfort and blessing are dependent on God's people returning not just to their own land but to the Lord himself (v. 3). Repentance is not a once-and-for-all, 'did it at my conversion' affair. It is a daily, hourly state of heart and mind, a turning away from our own wills towards God.

Prayer

Almighty God, if there is any area of my life where I have departed from your word, please help me to see it, repent and return to your perfect plan for me. Amen

JO

A city without walls

I looked up and saw a man with a measuring line in his hand. Then I asked, 'Where are you going?' He answered me, 'To measure Jerusalem, to see what is its width and what is its length.' Then the angel who talked with me came forward, and another angel came forward to meet him, and said to him, 'Run, say to that young man: Jerusalem shall be inhabited like villages without walls, because of the multitude of people and animals in it. For I will be a wall of fire all around it, says the Lord, and I will be the glory within it.'

The concepts of counting and measuring are interesting ones in scripture. Sometimes we are encouraged to count up and measure what God has done (see, for example, Psalm 48:12–14) and sometimes the act of reducing the work of the Lord to mere numbers on a page is considered to be a sin against his goodness (see 2 Samuel 24).

This second chapter of Zechariah explores that dichotomy. One would have thought that, in order to rebuild the city of Jerusalem, it would be necessary to make careful plans. How much can we hope to achieve? What supplies do we have? Can we do just this bit or can we stretch to cover that area as well? However, the vision that Zechariah receives from God takes a different approach. Yes, this is an earthly city and, indeed, Nehemiah will arrive in a few years' time and head up the work of rebuilding the walls of the earthly

Jerusalem. Jerusalem, though, is also a picture, a symbol, of the place where God will dwell with his people—Jews and Gentiles, men and women. It is the place without walls, but where his people will live in safety and his glory will be for all eternity.

Spend some time today meditating on this picture and compare it to the life of the local church. Are we creating communities that are like 'villages without walls' or are we restricting the work of God by building walls around what we do and keeping people out?

Prayer

Heavenly Father, I commit myself today to building your Church in my community—a place without walls, where all those you are calling can meet with you and share your life.

JO

ZECHARIAH 3:1–4, 8–9 (NRSV, ABRIDGED)

I will clothe you

Then he showed me the high priest Joshua standing before the angel of the Lord, and Satan standing at his right hand to accuse him... Now Joshua was dressed with filthy clothes as he stood before the angel. The angel said to those who were standing before him, 'Take off his filthy clothes.' And to him he said, 'See, I have taken your guilt away from you, and I will clothe you with festal apparel... Now listen, Joshua, high priest, you and your colleagues who sit before you! For they are an omen of things to come: I am going to bring my servant the Branch... and I will remove the guilt of this land in a single day.'

The priests' ceremonial duties required them to adhere to a strict diet, avoid contamination and strive for perfection in keeping the Law of the Lord. The high priest in particular had a duty to keep himself clean before God. He had the privilege of appearing before the Lord on behalf of the people; how could he do that if he was unclean? However, then Zechariah hears the Lord informing Satan that Joshua is 'a brand plucked from the fire' (v. 2) and also telling Joshua that his guilt has been removed. Joshua's old clothes are removed and replaced, not just with clean clothes but with 'festal apparel'. Joshua was told, too, that the Lord was going to bring 'my servant the Branch', the perfect high priest, who would mediate between God and men and women. Some 500 years before the time of Jesus, God has revealed that his purposes are

already in place to deal with sin.

Zechariah lived under the old covenant, with its demand for sacrifices, its laws and solemn Day of Atonement. Here he glimpsed the new covenant, the good news that God will deal with sin once and for all in the Messiah. All those who repent will have their sin removed. Paul writes: 'As many of you as were baptized into Christ have clothed yourselves with Christ' (Galatians 3:27). Jesus himself is our high priest, our clean clothes and the reason for our acceptance by God.

Meditation

When Satan tempts me to despair,
and tells me of the guilt within,
Upward I look and see him there
who made an end to all my sin.

Charitie L. Bancroft (1841–1923)

JO

By my Spirit

The angel... came again, and wakened me, as one is wakened from sleep. He said to me, 'What do you see?' And I said, 'I see a lamp-stand all of gold, with a bowl on the top of it; there are seven lamps on it, with seven lips on each of the lamps that are on the top of it. And by it there are two olive trees, one on the right of the bowl and the other on its left.' I said to the angel... 'What are these, my lord?'... He said to me, 'This is the word of the Lord to Zerubbabel: Not by might, nor by power, but by my spirit, says the Lord of hosts.'

Three men dedicated themselves to returning to Jerusalem, rebuilding the temple and re-establishing the nation of Israel. Joshua was the high priest, responsible for spiritual health; Zerubbabel was the governor, responsible for temporal affairs and the work of rebuilding; and Zechariah was the prophet, bringing the word of God.

Now, we see in these verses Zechariah being shown a vision of a lamp with seven bowls of oil and two olive trees and, when he enquires about its meaning, he is given, not a detailed explanation, but a word from God—not for the high priest, nor even for himself, but for Zerubbabel, the governor—as it were, the man with the pencil behind his ear and the clipboard in his hand: 'Not by might, not by power, but by my spirit, says the Lord of hosts.'

In Acts 6:3, we read that even those appointed to wait on tables were to be 'full of the Spirit'. In any work for God, the spiritual leader and the prophet need to be filled with the Spirit of God, but, we learn here, so do those who are called to fulfil roles behind the scenes.

There is a never-ending supply of the oil of the Spirit and the word of the Lord reminds us that human efforts alone can never accomplish his work. If we truly want to extend his Kingdom and tell the world of his love, we must understand that these things can only be done through the power of the Holy Spirit.

Meditation

For none can guess its grace, till he become the place wherein the Holy Spirit makes his dwelling.

Bianco of Siena, 15th century, translated in 1867

JO

Dealing with sin

Again I looked up and saw a flying scroll... Then he [the angel] said to me, 'This is the curse that goes out over the face of the whole land; for everyone who steals shall be cut off according to the writing on one side, and everyone who swears falsely shall be cut off according to the writing on the other side. I have sent it out, says the Lord of hosts, and it shall enter the house of the thief, and the house of anyone who swears falsely by my name; and it shall abide in that house and consume it, both timber and stones.' Then the angel ... came forward and said to me, 'Look up and see what this is that is coming out.' I said, 'What is it?' He said, 'This is a basket coming out.' And he said, 'This is their iniquity in all the land.' Then a leaden cover was lifted, and there was a woman sitting in the basket! And he said, 'This is Wickedness.'

These visions are messages for the people returning to the land. Homes would be established, families begun and commerce set in motion. God has something to say to those engaged in these activities.

First, he shows Zechariah a flying scroll. Not a quiet verse from scripture, read in private or in the temple, but a banner in the sky—absolutely clear to everyone. The message is, 'The commandments given through Moses still apply: don't steal or bear false witness. When you steal and lie, you destroy trust and relationships.'

The next vision is of a basket—a measuring tool in the marketplace in those times—containing a woman. She depicts evil—perhaps evil in the world of commerce and trade. Here, too, trust, honesty and integrity are required. Zechariah hears the angel say that she will be removed to a place prepared for her (see vv. 9–11).

We can only guess at the meanings of these visions, but the underlying message seems clear: God will not tolerate sin. He requires that his people live in righteousness and truth with one another. We need to repent of any sin today so that our homes, families and workplaces will be pleasing to him.

Prayer

'Have mercy on me, O God, according to your steadfast love... Wash me thoroughly from my iniquity, and cleanse me from my sin'
(Psalm 51:1–2).

JO

Zechariah 6:9–13 (NRSV, abridged)

King and priest

The word of the Lord came to me: Collect silver and gold from the exiles… who have arrived from Babylon; and go the same day to the house of Josiah son of Zephaniah. Take the silver and gold and make a crown, and set it on the head of the high priest Joshua son of Jehozadak; say to him: Thus says the Lord of hosts: Here is a man whose name is Branch: for he shall branch out in his place, and he shall build the temple of the Lord… he shall bear royal honour, and shall sit and rule on his throne.

Prophetic sight is not a complete and clear picture of what is going to happen and when. It is more like a collection of images—a scrapbook, a verse of eloquent poetry, a handful of evocative photographs, a dream or an abstract painting. We have to study the poetry and the photographs, think about the dream and pore over the painting.

Zechariah's next vision contained concepts that would have puzzled him and the other returning exiles very much. He was instructed to crown the high priest and also told that 'those who are far off shall come and help to build the temple of the Lord' (v. 15). Now, the office of the high priest was never combined with that of the king and those not born into the Jewish faith could never have a hand in building the temple of God.

However, we who live under the new covenant know that Jesus the Messiah is both our high priest and sacrificial lamb; and our king and the suffering servant. Under his rule all who draw near to him—whether Jew or Gentile—can help to build his kingdom.

Here is a young man being shown the truth about the Messiah 500 years before the birth of Jesus. Let's rejoice today that we do not have to rely on a human priest to intercede for us. Let's rejoice that we belong to a kingdom the ruler of which is absolute love and absolute truth and we, unworthy as we are, can help to build his Church in the world today.

Prayer

A great High Priest whose name is Love, who ever lives and pleads for me… The King of glory and of grace! One with himself I cannot die…

Charitie L. Bancroft (1841–1923)

JO

Was it for me?

Then the word of the Lord of hosts came to me: Say to all the people of the land and the priests: When you fasted and lamented in the fifth month and in the seventh, for these seventy years, was it for me that you fasted? And when you eat and when you drink, do you not eat and drink only for yourselves? Were not these the words that the Lord proclaimed by the former prophets, when Jerusalem was inhabited and in prosperity…? … Thus says the Lord of hosts: Render true judgments, show kindness and mercy to one another; do not oppress the widow, the orphan, the alien, or the poor; and do not devise evil in your hearts against one another.

Two years have passed and, as more exiles arrive back from Babylon and the rebuilding of the temple gets into its stride, there are details about life and worship that need to be sorted out. Verse 2 tells how a delegation is sent from Bethel, about 12 miles from Jerusalem, to get a ruling on the matter of fasting.

After the destruction of Jerusalem, both those in exile and those who remained in the land established days of remembrance. They fasted and mourned for their lost temple and their lost way of life. Jeremiah's songs of despair in Lamentations might well have been their hymnbook then. Now they want to know whether or not they should continue the practice.

Their question provokes a series of messages from God through Zechariah in chapters 7 and 8. When Jesus came, he also tended not to answer questions directly but encouraged a new way of looking at things. Think of the rich young man in Matthew 19 who came to him with a simple query about eternal life and was confronted with the need to invest his money quite differently. There was also the lawyer in Luke 10 who asked about eternal life and was challenged to love the unlovable.

In Zechariah 7, the visitors from Bethel were no doubt challenged by the response they received: 'It doesn't matter whether you fast or feast,' says the Lord. 'What matters is how you live and treat one another.'

Prayer

Almighty God, in this time of Lent, challenge me again with the need to live according to your word and in the light of your law of love. Amen

JO

'Let us go with you'

Thus says the Lord of hosts: Peoples shall yet come, the inhabitants of many cities; the inhabitants of one city shall go to one another, saying, 'Come, let us go to entreat the favour of the Lord, and to seek the Lord of hosts; I myself am going.' Many peoples and strong nations shall come to seek the Lord of hosts in Jerusalem, and to entreat the favour of the Lord. Thus says the Lord of hosts: In those days ten men from nations of every language shall take hold of a Jew, grasping his garment and saying, 'Let us go with you, for we have heard that God is with you.'

So often in scripture the words of the poets and prophets have 'now' and 'in those times' applications. So it is here. The Lord is encouraging and uplifting. He tells his people how much he loves them, how he wants to live among them (see vv. 2–8). He speaks of the difficulties they have gone through and promises that, if they 'let their hands be strong' (v. 9), he will indeed bless both those who remained in the desolate land and those he will bring back from exile.

Also, the Lord finally gives his answer to the question the people asked him about fasting, assuring them that their remembrance day observances are to be 'seasons of joy and gladness' (v. 19), but only if they continue to love truth and peace.

Then, in the final section, comes that phrase 'in those days', and the prophetic telescope is focused on the future. The people were anxious to re-establish their nation, rebuild the temple and restore the purity of their worship and service to God. So, we might what they made of Zechariah's description of the day coming when people from many cities and nations would come to seek the Lord.

That is what God did in Jesus and we have grasped hold of the truths in the Jewish faith and found their Messiah to be our Saviour, too. Let's make ourselves available for others who want to 'entreat the favour of the Lord'.

Prayer

Heavenly Father, may those I meet today know that you are with me and may I in some way help them on their journey to faith. Amen

JO

Your king is coming!

Rejoice greatly, O daughter Zion! Shout aloud, O daughter Jerusalem! Lo, your king comes to you; triumphant and victorious is he, humble and riding on a donkey, on a colt, the foal of a donkey. He will cut off the chariot from Ephraim and the war horse from Jerusalem; and the battle bow shall be cut off, and he shall command peace to the nations; his dominion shall be from sea to sea, and from the River to the ends of the earth... Because of the blood of my covenant with you, I will set your prisoners free from the waterless pit. Return to your stronghold, O prisoners of hope; today I declare that I will restore to you double... I will arouse your sons, O Zion... and wield you like a warrior's sword.

Almost 20 years have passed. Zechariah is older, with more experience of the goodness and faithfulness of God. The last six chapters of his book contain two 'oracles', or messages, that God gave to him at that point.

When we view mountains from a distance, they may appear to be close together, but, when we approach them, we realize that they are separated by deep valleys. So it is with prophecy. Zechariah's words concerning the events of his time are set against his prophecies concerning the Messiah's coming and they are mixed with messages about the end of time, when the Messiah's 'dominion shall be from sea to sea' (v. 10). Those events were separated by thousands of years, but that does not make them any less true.

Some 200 years after Zechariah,

Alexander the Great fulfilled his words regarding the nations surrounding Israel. The prophecy in verse 9 was fulfilled by Jesus' entry into Jerusalem—an event recorded in all four Gospels (see Matthew 21:1–9; Mark 11:1–11; Luke 19: 28–44 and John 12:12–19). As a result, we can be confident that the future application of these prophetic words will also come to pass. There will come a time when the Messiah himself shall 'command peace to the nations' (v. 10) and the people of God, like the jewels of a crown, 'shall shine on his land' (v. 16).

Prayer

Almighty God, I thank you that you are working your purposes out in the world and in your time all that you have promised will come to pass.
Amen

JO

'I will bring them back'

I will strengthen the house of Judah, and I will save the house of Joseph. I will bring them back because I have compassion on them, and they shall be as though I had not rejected them; for I am the Lord their God and I will answer them. Then the people of Ephraim shall become like warriors, and their hearts shall be glad as with wine. Their children shall see it and rejoice, their hearts shall exult in the Lord... I will bring them home... until there is no room for them.

As Zechariah continues to speak the message from God, words of encouragement and hope pour out of him. Chapter 10 is rich with the love of God for his people. Over and over again he promises good things to them—'I will… I will… I will.'

There are days when we need to hear words of warning from God, but today the words are all of love and encouragement, consolation and promise: 'I will do all these things for my people.'

In the years before the overthrow and exile of the people of Israel, Jeremiah was sent to call the people to repentance. His prophetic words described how God feels when his people go their own way: he feels like a husband whose wife has committed adultery. Even at that moment, though, he assured his people, 'I will heal your faithlessness' (Jeremiah 3:22). Are you feeling weak today or sorry or lacking in faith and

love? God can restore you. He can heal whatever it is that has spoilt your relationship with him and strengthen you for the future.

Zechariah begins this chapter with a lovely word picture. In verse 1, he says, 'Ask rain from the Lord in the season of the spring rain.' If a seed is planted in the ground, then the ground needs to be warmed and watered in order for the seed to sprout and grow. You have been 'planted' into the kingdom of God. Pray today for the rain of his blessing to help you grow.

Prayer

Almighty God, I thank you for your great love. Forgive my sins, restore me to your presence, bless me with strength and courage and heal my faithlessness. I ask it in the name of Jesus. Amen

JO

Thirty shekels of silver

I became the shepherd of the flock doomed to slaughter. I took two staffs; one I named Favour, the other I named Unity, and I tended the sheep. In one month I disposed of the three shepherds, for I had become impatient with them, and they also detested me. So I said, 'I will not be your shepherd. What is to die, let it die; what is to be destroyed, let it be destroyed; and let those that are left devour the flesh of one another! … I then said to [the sheep merchants], 'If it seems right to you, give me my wages; but if not, keep them.' So they weighed out as my wages thirty shekels of silver.

The Old Testament prophets were often told to speak out the words God gave them. Sometimes they were also told to act out the message. Here, Zechariah is told to get a job as a shepherd—doing the job on behalf of a butcher (v. 4).

The warm, comforting words of the last chapter have gone and Zechariah is now acting out the bitter words of the Lord: 'I will not be your shepherd.' There is to come a time when his favour will have gone, the unity of the nation will have been destroyed and the people left to the mercies of a 'worthless shepherd' (v .15). What does Zechariah have to show for his bitter portrayal of judgment? Just 30 shekels of silver—the price of a damaged slave (see Exodus 21:32). It is also the price of betrayal and death (see Matthew 27:3–5).

God had brought the people back to their own land and assured them of his presence among them, but knew that they would still rebel, still set themselves against his way and eventually reject the good shepherd himself. The covenant would be broken and their unity destroyed.

Consider for a while the lonely figure of Zechariah, called to act out the part of a worthless shepherd (see v. 15). If you have any leadership responsibility, teaching ministry or authority in the Church, then pray that God will strengthen you to be a faithful shepherd of his people.

Meditation

'Not many of you should become teachers, my brothers and sisters, for you know that we who teach will be judged with greater strictness'
(James 3:1).

JO

The one they pierced

On that day the Lord will shield the inhabitants of Jerusalem so that the feeblest among them on that day shall be like David, and the house of David shall be like God, like the angel of the Lord, at their head. And on that day I will seek to destroy all the nations that come against Jerusalem. And I will pour out a spirit of compassion and supplication on the house of David and the inhabitants of Jerusalem, so that, when they look on the one whom they have pierced, they shall mourn for him, as one mourns for an only child, and weep bitterly over him, as one weeps over a firstborn... On that day a fountain shall be opened for the house of David and the inhabitants of Jerusalem, to cleanse them from sin and impurity.

Here, in another oracle given to Zechariah, we hear God commit himself to protecting and blessing Jerusalem, so that the weakest inhabitant of that city will be stronger even than the great king, David.

Once again we hear the phrase 'on that day'—the time when he will pour out on his people a spirit of compassion and supplication as each tribe, each family, each person will be in mourning (see vv. 12–14). Did Zechariah puzzle over those words—'they shall look on him whom they have pierced'—and wonder what they referred to?

God is going to restore his covenant relationship with Israel and it will ultimately be achieved through Jesus, the Messiah. The first verse of chapter 13 would seem to fit better as the finale for chapter 12 for a fountain was indeed opened on the day that Christ died and his blood cleansed us from all sin.

In the last act of history, the circle of salvation will be completed as God will bring his people into his eternal kingdom. The centre of that kingdom will be the new Jerusalem (Revelation 21:10) and the promises of God for the city and its inhabitants will finally be fulfilled.

Prayer

Almighty God, I thank and praise you that you continue to work your purposes out. Whatever my world looks like today, help me to look forward to the new heaven and the new earth and worship you—Lord of the past, present and future. Amen

JO

The Lord is our God

On that day, says the Lord of hosts, I will cut off the names of the idols from the lands, so that they shall be remembered no more; and also I will remove from the land the prophets and the unclean spirit. And if any prophets appear again, their fathers and mothers who bore them will say to them, 'You shall not live, for you speak lies in the name of the Lord.'… 'Awake, O sword, against my shepherd, against the man who is my associate,' says the Lord of hosts. Strike the shepherd, that the sheep may be scattered… In the whole land, says the Lord, two-thirds shall be cut off and perish, and one-third shall be left alive. And I will put this third into the fire, refine them as one refines silver… They will call on my name, and I will answer them. I will say, 'They are my people'; and they will say, 'The Lord is our God.'

Now God turns from the individual repentance and cleansing of chapter 12 to the cleansing of society itself, washing away idolatry and false prophecy. How will that be accomplished? First, there is the responsibility we each carry to ensure that the society we live in is pleasing to God. We may well be called to take action ourselves when we see God's instructions set aside.

Second, we have the picture of the stricken shepherd, wounded by his friends. Christ himself had those verses in mind as he walked with his friends to Gethsemane, anticipating the blow that would fell him and scatter his disciples (Matthew 26:31). However, that blow made it possible for a remnant to survive and form the start of the new kingdom.

Third, we have the process of refining. Repentance and cleansing are the start, then come times of learning, testing, discipline. What is God's ultimate purpose in this cleansing process? It is so that he can say of us, 'They are my people' and we can say, 'The Lord is our God.' We belong to him. He belongs to us. We are family. We are one.

Prayer

Almighty God, creator and sustainer of the universe, I rejoice today that I am part of you and you are part of me. Show me day by day more of what that means. Amen

JO

King over all the earth

On that day his feet shall stand on the Mount of Olives, which lies before Jerusalem on the east; and the Mount of Olives shall be split in two from east to west by a very wide valley; so that one half of the Mount shall withdraw northwards, and the other half southwards... Then the Lord my God will come, and all the holy ones with him. On that day there shall not be either cold or frost. And there shall be continuous day... And the Lord will become king over all the earth; on that day the Lord will be one and his name one.

In Acts 1, we read of the last moments of Jesus' presence on earth. His disciples believed that he was the Messiah and they would have recalled all that they had learned from the prophets of old about the Messiah. As they stood there with him, they may have remembered these words from Zechariah. Was that the moment the mountain would split in two? Would they be caught up to heaven with him? Were the enemies of Israel about to be defeated? Was Jesus about to become king over all the earth? So they asked him excitedly, 'Lord, is this the time when you will restore the kingdom to Israel?' (v. 6).

Jesus, however, gently but firmly, tells them that it is not for them to know exactly when that will happen. The important thing for them was that the Holy Spirit was going to give them the power to witness to what they had seen and ensure that men, women and children everywhere would have the opportunity to hear the good news of Jesus Christ and respond to him.

As we read this final chapter of Zechariah, let us, too, rejoice in the promises of his glorious coming and look forward with longing to the day when there will be no night and everything on earth will be redeemed and made holy by him. Let's commit ourselves to bringing that day nearer by being obedient to his call, faithful in prayer and declaring whenever we can the reality of his saving power now.

Prayer

Holy Spirit, who inspired Zechariah with these words of prophecy, warning and encouragement, inspire me also with the ability to understand his message and apply it to my own life and times. Amen

JO

1 Corinthians 13

'The Greeks have a word for it.' Well, in this case, they have several words for it—all meaning 'love' in one form or another. There is *eros*, sexual love; there is *phileo*, to like something or someone; and there is the noblest form of love, *agape*. This chapter is about the last, which the Christians borrowed to describe the love of God and the self-giving love that Jesus showed for us. Then, because Christ calls us to love as we are loved, it was applied to the deep love that Christ's followers are meant to practise. This wonderful chapter of 1 Corinthians—surely one of the best-loved passages in the Bible— is about *agape* love, which makes it doubly strange that the translators of the King James Bible rendered it as 'charity'.

It is important to read this chapter in its context. It doesn't simply emerge as a new topic in Paul's thinking. He had been dealing with the issue of spiritual gifts in the church at Corinth, urging them to seek and use them wisely and so that they would be a blessing for the whole fellowship. Prophecy, healing, tongues and their interpretation—he went through several lists of the life-enhancing gifts of the Spirit. He was writing to a church that was already pretty gifted, from what we can deduce from his words, so we can imagine how they felt when he told them that he was going to tell them about the most 'excellent' gift of all. What could it possibly be?

The answer soon became clear: love! As he warms to his subject, the apostle becomes positively poetic. Anyone who thinks of Paul as a tight-lipped misogynist would be forced to revise their opinion having read this passage. This is a man who knows how to love and be loved. As these words are read out at weddings, I sometimes feel like shouting out, 'This is Paul, remember!' His magnificent hymn to love is deeper, truer to human experience, higher in its vision of intimacy and self-giving than anything else I can think of in literature.

Agape is a beautiful word for a beautiful idea. When a couple exchange rings in the marriage service they say, 'All that I am I give to you'. The 'other' is infinitely precious. That is love; that is *agape* love. That is the love of God revealed in human experience, which is precisely what this chapter is all about.

David Winter

1 CORINTHIANS 13:1–2 (NRSV)

The greatest gift

If I speak in the tongues of mortals and of angels, but do not have love, I am a noisy gong or a clanging cymbal. And if I have prophetic powers, and understand all mysteries and all knowledge, and if I have all faith, so as to remove mountains, but do not have love, I am nothing.

We need to read the last part of the preceding chapter to get the full impact of Paul's words here. He had been writing to the Corinthians about the gifts of the Spirit, which are to be exercised by Christians 'for the common good' (12:7). These gifts cover an enormous range—wisdom, knowledge, faith, healing, tongues, prophecy. Clearly the apostle recognizes the value of these gifts in the life of the Church, though he seems anxious that, in some cases, they are being misused or wrongly applied. Yet, they are, for him, true marks of a Spirit-filled church and evidence of spiritual life.

So, when he spoke of something that is better, 'more excellent', greater than the greatest of gifts, they must have wondered what on earth he could mean. These verses would have come like a bombshell. You claim to speak in tongues (whether human languages or the language of angels)? Fine, but, if you do not have the gift of love, your words are as valueless as a noisy gong or a clanging cymbal. If

the gift you practise is prophecy (a gift Paul highly praised: see 14:24–25), knowledge or 'faith' of the kind that 'moves mountains', that's also fine, but, if your gift isn't infused with love, then you are 'nothing'. Without love, even the most spectacular gifts are worthless.

In two of the most telling sentences in any of his letters, the apostle hammers home his priorities. The first 'fruit' of the Spirit, he told the church at Galatia, is 'love' (Galatians 5:22). It follows, then, that where the gifts of the same Spirit are being exercised, the motivation and the outcome of that exercise must be love. Without it, these gifts become silly toys, mere spiritual pyrotechnics. As he states just a sentence or so before our passages: 'Strive for the greater gifts' (1 Corinthians 12:31).

Reflection

Clanging gongs and noisy cymbals—that is Paul's valuation of a religious life without love.

DW

Greater than sacrificial giving

If I give away all my possessions, and if I hand over my body so that I may boast, but do not have love, I gain nothing.

In this splendid piece of rhetoric (which shows that Paul was familiar with all the skills of classical oratory), he continues to use the first person ('I') and pursue his argument even further. To give, and to give generously, is a Christian virtue, which Paul emphasizes in a later letter to the same church. In 2 Corinthians 9:1–7, he expands the point at length, concluding, 'God loves a cheerful giver' (v. 7). To be rid of 'all my possessions' was exactly what Jesus demanded of the rich young ruler (Luke 18:22). Surely that would be evidence of total devotion?

Even more striking, of course, would be the sacrifice of my own life—martyrdom, in fact. The traditional translation is 'hand over my body to be burned'—NRSV bases its rather obscure rendering on a different Greek text. In both cases, though, the meaning is the same. Even the offering of my very life, freely laid down for the cause of Christ (or, sadly, to gain some spiritual kudos), is 'nothing' if I do not have love.

The repetition of 'nothing' is very powerful. It means more than

that the gesture is meaningless or the giver useless. Notice that Paul does not says 'it' is nothing, but 'I' am. As Jerome Murphy O'Connor points out in his commentary on this book (*The People's Bible Commentary: 1 Corinthians*, BRF, 1997), 'Paul means that without love we do not exist'.

The reference to burning the body is a strange one. Of course, many Christians in the first centuries of the Church were burnt at the stake—Bishop Polycarp of Smyrna among them—but those executions were much later than this letter of Paul's. He may have had in mind a famous tomb in Athens where an Indian was buried who had burnt himself to death in pursuit of immortality. The detail is, in any case, unimportant. The message is clear: sacrificial giving, whether of possessions or even my own life, is an empty gesture without love.

Reflection

Sacrificial love is greater than sacrificial giving, though, often, as with Jesus, the one inevitably leads to the other.

DW

The nature of love

Love is patient; love is kind; love is not envious or boastful or arrogant or rude. It does not insist on its own way; it is not irritable or resentful; it does not rejoice in wrongdoing, but rejoices in the truth. It bears all things, believes all things, hopes all things, endures all things.

Paul has told us, in no uncertain terms, about the consequences of the absence of love. He now sets out, in equally memorable language, to tell us what love is and what it is not. It's no wonder that this passage is often read at marriage services, for there can be no more eloquent and comprehensive summary of the qualities of this elusive virtue than what the apostle offers here.

Paul spells out seven distinctive characteristics of love: it is patient, kind, rejoices in the truth, bears all things, believes all things, hopes all things and endures all things. He also spells out eight characteristics that it does *not* have: it is not envious, boastful, arrogant, rude, self-assertive, irritable, resentful or rejoicing in wrongdoing. It's immediately obvious that several of these are simple opposites—patient versus irritable, rejoicing in the truth versus rejoicing in wrongdoing. It's also obvious how the positives are attractive qualities (kind, trusting, hopeful) and the negatives are ugly (arrogant, boastful, self-assertive). 'Rude' is a strange word to find

here. The actual word Paul used means 'indecent' or 'unseemly', and suggests a tendency to inappropriate behaviour or speech—perhaps even a delight in shocking people. The word translated as 'resentful' carries the sense of keeping a record of wrongs—true love is more willing to wipe the slate of memory clean.

It might seem that Paul pictures love as soft and gullible ('bears all things, believes all things, hopes all things'), but, in fact, he is speaking of 'endurance'. Love is infinitely strong and, therefore, can't be lightly deflected from its path of courage, trust and hope. That is the source of its strength.

Reflection

There have been many popular films that have tried to encapsulate what love is all about, but I am not sure how often the writers have had this passage in mind. Nevertheless, it's a helpful exercise to go through this chapter and list what Paul says love is and then to use it for self-examination.

DW

1 Corinthians 13:8–10 (NRSV)

Love never ends

Love never ends. But as for prophecies, they will come to an end; as for tongues, they will cease; as for knowledge, it will come to an end. For we know only in part, and we prophesy only in part; but when the complete comes, the partial will come to an end.

It's just as simple and straightforward in Paul's Greek as it is in our English: 'love never ends'. Yet, these words express one of the most profound truths of human experience. True love, *agape* love, love that gives rather than demands, can never end. Circumstances can't change it. Time can't touch it. Death doesn't end it, as anyone who has lost a loved one knows.

The whole principle flows from another great declaration of the New Testament: 'God is love'. If love is of the very nature of God, if it's what he is, in his character and being, then, as John writes in the first of his letters, 'those who abide in love abide in God, and God abides in them' (1 John 4:16). Love can never end because God never ends.

In contrast, all the other great spiritual gifts that the Corinthian Christians so prized are time-dated. One day, prophecy will pass its sell-by date. You can't prophesy when the events have actually taken place. One day, tongues will be stilled. We shall speak to God and God will speak to us face to face:

'The throne of God and of the Lamb will be in it [the heavenly city], and his servants will worship him; they will see his face, and his name will be on their foreheads' (Revelation 22:3–4). Knowledge, human and divine, will come to an end because, in the purposes of God, all will be revealed in shining truth. Consequently, the other gifts fall into the category of 'partial', to be rendered redundant when the 'complete' is revealed. We know in part and prophesy in part until the day when God's revelation is clear to everyone.

To return to the key phrase 'Love never ends', though. Love has no terminal date, its value will never fade: 'Many waters cannot quench love, neither can floods drown it' (Song of Solomon 8:7).

Reflection

Prophecy will fade away,
Melting in the light of day;
Love will ever with us stay;
Therefore give us love.

Christopher Wordsworth (1807–85)
DW

1 Corinthians 13:11 (NRSV)

On to maturity

When I was a child, I spoke like a child, I thought like a child, I reasoned like a child; when I became an adult, I put an end to childish ways.

Many years ago, I was speaking to a group of nurses at a big London teaching hospital. I was talking about maturity and suggested that an important moment in their lives was probably when they threw away or passed on their favourite teddy bear. I could see that I had struck a chord, because they started whispering to each other and giggling. Eventually one of them spoke: 'The truth is, most of us have still got our teddy bears. They're tucked up in bed in the nurses' home waiting for us now.' Perhaps 'putting an end to childish ways' was more complicated than I had thought!

Maturity is a complicated issue. Watching my oldest grandchild approach the teen years, I realize afresh how complicated the transition from childhood to adult is. What is true in everyday human experience is also true in the life of the Christian disciple. Childish notions of God (as a kind of fairy godmother, granting our wishes, for instance, or a chess master pushing pawns around the board of life) can be hard to eradicate. Equally, a reluctance to accept responsibility for the consequences of our words and actions can show that we are still far from being mature Christians.

The point Paul is making is part of his whole argument about the priority of love over other gifts. It is childish to treat the gifts of the Spirit like Christmas presents and simply enjoy them for ourselves. That might have been all right during our adolescence as Christians, but maturity should bring the realization that gifts without love are empty toys. They are not gifts to the individual, but for the Church. Elsewhere, he calls the Corinthians 'infants in Christ' (3:1) and warns them not to be 'children in your thinking' (14:20). That is a call to grow up. It would be foolish to live for the present (and the presents!) rather than join those Paul has already dubbed 'the mature (2:6).

Reflection

The gifts of the Spirit are not an end in themselves, but aids to that maturity in love that reaches its completion in Christ.

DW

The undistorted vision

For now we see in a mirror, dimly, but then we will see face to face. Now I know only in part; then I will know fully, even as I have been fully known.

In Roman times, mirrors were not made of glass, but polished metal. They did not give very true or accurate images—shaving or applying make-up must have been a tricky business! Corinth was known for manufacturing these mirrors, but even the best ones offered an imperfect reflection. When Paul speaks of seeing 'in a mirror, dimly', therefore, he is talking of a distorted vision of ourselves or anyone else. That was how he saw the Christian's present relationship with God: clouded, partial, incomplete.

We know neither ourselves truly nor God. That limitation we must accept as part of our humanity. As the opening prologue of John's Gospel puts it, 'No one has ever seen God' (1: 18). Many had sought to do so, from Moses (Exodus 33:18–20) to the apostle Philip (John 14:8–9), but the glory of the eternal God is not for mortal eyes, except in the human form of Jesus.

This incomplete vision is not everlasting, however. One day—the 'then' Paul mentions here—we shall see God 'face to face'. He who knows me perfectly, in every detail of my existence, will also reveal himself fully. At last, we shall understand all that was hitherto questions, doubts or difficulties. We shall know in the same way that God knows us—completely, graciously, lovingly.

When is this 'then', though? The most straightforward reading would be to assume that it is the second coming of Christ—an event that Paul and the early Church expected imminently. However, the context also suggests that it is when we attain 'maturity in love' (though the two might be the same, of course). Certainly the apostle wants his readers to have that maturity as a goal, with the undistorted heavenly vision as its reward. He who is Love can only truly be known through love.

Reflection
We are often aware of the dimness of the mirror in which we try to peruse the purposes of God. We are full of questions, hesitations, misgivings, even about matters of faith. The promise here is that one day we shall know. Until then, we trust.

DW

The greatest of these

And now faith, hope, and love abide, these three; and the greatest of these is love.

A key word in this sentence is 'abide': faith, hope and love 'abide'. It's not a word used much in modern English, but it speaks of putting down roots, having a permanent home, of 'dwelling', of an 'abode'. Jesus told his followers to 'abide' in him, to be rooted in him (John 15:4). So we could translate these words thus: 'Three things last for ever: faith, hope and love.' They are the fixed points of our very existence as Christians. Through faith we receive grace and forgiveness; through hope we know security and the promise of eternal life; through love we can encounter the God who is love.

Paul was the great apostle of faith—no one reading the letter to the Romans could doubt that! Equally, he preached the Christian hope, urging the followers of Christ to anchor their lives to the promises of God. Yet, in this final summary of his whole argument on the subject, he says, 'the greatest of these is love': it is greater than faith, greater than hope.

We might well ask why. After all, as we usually see it, love is a 'feeling', whereas faith and hope are actions of the will. I can't make myself love someone, not even God, but I can (it might seem) decide to believe and to hope. In fact, as the New Testament makes very clear, all three are gifts of God—gifts we can seek and pray for, but not demand. It is by the grace of God that we can believe and trust in him. It is by the grace of God that we can have that 'sure and certain hope' (in the old Prayer Book phrase) of eternal life. It is through the grace of God that we can love him and our neighbours.

Love is the 'greatest', surely, because it reflects the heart of God, who is love. Faith and hope bring us to the presence of God; love takes us into his very heart.

Reflection

Faith without love is cold, and hope without love is grim. Love is the fire which kindles faith and it is the light which turns hope into certainty.

William Barclay, *The Letters to the Corinthians* (St Andrew Press, 1957)

DW

Don't forget to renew your annual subscription to *New Daylight*! If you enjoy the notes, why not also consider giving a gift subscription to a friend or member of your family?

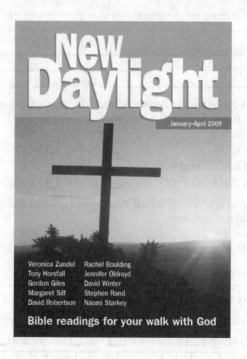

You will find a subscription order form overleaf.
New Daylight is also available from your local Christian bookshop.

SUBSCRIPTIONS

❏ Please send me a Bible reading resources pack to encourage Bible reading in my church

❏ I would like to take out a subscription myself (complete your name and address details only once)

❏ I would like to give a gift subscription (please complete both name and address sections below)

Your name _____

Your address _____

_____ Postcode _____

Gift subscription name _____

Gift subscription address _____

_____ Postcode _____

Please send *New Daylight* beginning with the May / September 2009 / January 2010 issue: (delete as applicable)

(please tick box)	UK	SURFACE	AIR MAIL
NEW DAYLIGHT	❏ £13.80	❏ £15.00	❏ £17.10
NEW DAYLIGHT 3-year sub	❏ £33.00		
NEW DAYLIGHT DELUXE	❏ £17.40	❏ £21.90	❏ £27.00

I would like to take out an annual subscription to *Quiet Spaces* beginning with the next available issue:

(please tick box)	UK	SURFACE	AIR MAIL
QUIET SPACES	❏ £16.95	❏ £18.45	❏ £20.85

Please complete the payment details below and send your coupon, with appropriate payment, to:
BRF, 15 The Chambers, Vineyard, Abingdon OX14 3FE.

Total enclosed £ _____ (cheques should be made payable to 'BRF')

Payment by cheque ❏ postal order ❏ Visa ❏ Mastercard ❏ Switch ❏

Card number: ☐☐☐☐ ☐☐☐☐ ☐☐☐☐ ☐☐☐☐

Expires: ☐☐☐☐ Security code ☐☐☐ Issue no (Switch): ☐☐☐☐

Signature (essential if paying by credit/Switch card) _____

BRF is a Registered Charity

Easter: Mark's story

It's Holy Week and we are going to be following the events as Mark tells them. Then, in the week after Easter, we shall consider some of the teaching that Jesus gave during Holy Week—his last will and testament to his disciples.

Mark was almost certainly the first to write all this down. His account is hasty rather than measured, written under pressure, marked by stark themes and abrupt action. There is an almost nervous energy as Jesus is followed from place to place. 'Immediately', 'Very early', 'the next day'—these are the linking words of Mark's version of the greatest story ever told.

He starts, 'The beginning of the good news about Jesus', yet one-third of this good news focuses on the last week of Jesus' life. It starts with the triumphal entry into Jerusalem and then disintegrates into the antagonism of religious leaders, arrest by soldiers under cover of darkness, an illegal trial with trumped-up charges, abandonment by his friends and a shockingly violent death.

My work with *Open Doors* means meeting persecuted Christians—those who, even now, fear the knock on the door in the middle of the night, face the reality of injustice inside and outside the law courts and live with the possibility of torture and murder. Mark wrote his Gospel for people exactly like them. I suspect that they find particular significance in the detail of how the one whose name provokes the persecution of his followers faced arrest, trial and death. Jesus does not require anything of his followers that he has not experienced himself.

Mark does not hide the fact that the disciples reacted badly to their fear. One betrays, others run away, the most famous denies his Lord. I suspect that this too was—and is—an encouragement to those facing the same fears. Of course, it doesn't end with death; it ends with life-giving, hope-inspiring, glorious resurrection.

Mark includes a curious detail: 'A young man, wearing nothing but a linen garment, was following Jesus. When they seized him, he fled naked, leaving his garment behind' (14:51–52). It's so personal that many believe Mark wrote his own experience into his story at this particular point.

That's the great thing about Easter: it becomes good news for us when we become part of the story of Jesus, who died and rose again.

Stephen Rand

Hosanna!

When they brought the colt to Jesus and threw their cloaks over it, he sat on it. Many people spread their cloaks on the road, while others spread branches they had cut in the fields. Those who went ahead and those who followed shouted, 'Hosanna!' 'Blessed is he who comes in the name of the Lord!' 'Blessed is the coming kingdom of our father David!' 'Hosanna in the highest heaven!' Jesus entered Jerusalem and went into the temple courts. He looked around at everything, but since it was already late, he went out to Bethany with the Twelve.

I love preaching on Palm Sunday! I remember getting off a plane at 6.30am after 24 hours of travel back from Afghanistan and preaching at the Scout parade service four hours later. If you can't get excited about this story of a spontaneous explosion of joyful worship, perhaps you prefer not getting excited in church at all!

The story has its absurdities, of course. Observing worship always makes it look stranger than when you are part of it. I'm sure the people spreading their cloaks on the road for a man to ride over on a donkey thought it absolutely sensible behaviour.

Then there were the branches. They are a link to the feast of Tabernacles, when the people remembered God's provision for them. That's where the hymn they sang came from (see Psalm 118). They picked up an ancient liturgy and made it the basis of a worship that was spontaneous and creative.

'Hosanna' means 'save us now'. Maybe they thought that this was the Messiah coming to conquer, to turn out the detested Roman occupying power. It's hard to imagine that any guessed Jesus would die for their salvation just a few days later.

Note the contrast between the trappings of triumph accorded to an all-conquering king and the humility of a man riding on a donkey. God always triumphs in and through weakness rather than power.

How did Jesus react to this momentous, exhilarating experience? He went to the temple and he observed. Perhaps he was noting a different contrast—that between religious formalism and enthusiastic worship.

Prayer

Loving Father, prompt us to celebrate the salvation that comes through Jesus and worship you with spontaneous and creative joyfulness.

SR

Cleansing the temple

On reaching Jerusalem, Jesus entered the temple courts and began driving out those who were buying and selling there. He overturned the tables of the money changers and the benches of those selling doves, and would not allow anyone to carry merchandise through the temple courts. And as he taught them, he said, 'Is it not written: "My house will be called a house of prayer for all nations"? But you have made it "a den of robbers".' The chief priests and the teachers of the law heard this and began looking for a way to kill him, for they feared him, because the whole crowd was amazed at his teaching.

In Mark's Gospel, this incident is juxtaposed very clearly with the triumphal entry into Jerusalem. Jesus had looked around (v. 11) and had not much liked what he'd seen. One day he was being hailed as the one who will save; the next he was taking on the religious establishment. The temple was the pinnacle of organized religion—and it was rotten at its heart. It had been corrupted by the worship of the main human alternative to the true God: money, whose twin servants, selfishness and greed, held sway.

Jesus was outraged and took decisive action. What we see is not gentle Jesus, meek and mild; this is holy Jesus, unable to compromise on sin whatever shape it takes. When was the last time wrongdoing and injustice provoked us into action on behalf of the weak and the vulnerable?

Notice the reaction of the religious establishment. Jesus would have to go, he was dangerous—at least, dangerous to their status and privilege, which was built into the system.

I have a confession to make: I share society's suspicion of religion. Religion has caused countless wars; religion has been the excuse for prejudice and hatred; religion has inoculated generation after generation against the real thing—a living, dynamic relationship with Jesus Christ.

Notice, too, how Mark indicates that the whole crowd was amazed at his teaching. Perhaps that was because they had never seen truth expressed in action against injustice and exploitation. Teaching that leads to action for justice? That's not religion, that's amazing.

Prayer

Lord, save me from the corruption of empty religion and the love of money.

SR

Authority

While Jesus was walking in the temple courts, the chief priests, the teachers of the law and the elders came to him. 'By what authority are you doing these things?' they asked. 'And who gave you authority to do this?' Jesus replied, 'I will ask you one question… John's baptism—was it from heaven, or of human origin? Tell me!' They discussed it among themselves and said, 'If we say, "From heaven", he will ask, "Then why didn't you believe him?" But if we say, "Of human origin"…' (They feared the people, for everyone held that John really was a prophet.) So they answered Jesus, 'We don't know.' Jesus said, 'Neither will I tell you by what authority I am doing these things.'

Yesterday, Jesus cleaned up the place where his Father was worshipped and we read how that made the religious leaders want to kill him. So, today, they concoct a cunning plan. They are going to try and provoke Jesus into saying clearly what he has been implying with every action.

He allowed the people to make way for his entry into Jerusalem; he accepted their worship without hesitation; he exerted authority over the commercial activities in the temple. Who does he think he is? Not a hard question to answer.

They devise their catch question. If asked to name his authority for this kind of direct action, he'll have to say 'God' (because no one else can give him this kind of permission) and then they will have him: blasphemy. Just as helpful, the Romans won't be overly impressed by his denial of their authority.

Jesus, however, was only going to make public statements about being God's Son at a time and place of his choosing. That's the kind of authority he has. So, he returned their question with a question of his own. Yesterday the tables were overturned; today, they are just turned. Now his questioners are caught in a dilemma of their own. It is now their answer that risks inflaming the people, so they choose to sit on the fence and simply reply 'Don't know'. Jesus refused to give them the answer they wanted.

Reflection

'Jesus said, "All authority in heaven and on earth has been given to me"'
(Matthew 28:18). It is Jesus'
authority that calls us to live for him.

SR

This is my body

While they were eating, Jesus took bread, and when he had given thanks, he broke it and gave it to his disciples, saying, 'Take it; this is my body.' Then he took the cup, and when he had given thanks, he gave it to them, and they all drank from it. 'This is my blood of the covenant, which is poured out for many,' he said to them. 'Truly I tell you, I will not drink again of the fruit of the vine until that day when I drink it new in the kingdom of God.'

Mark's account of the first Eucharist is terse. In fact, the focus is on the identity of the one who would betray Jesus (see vv. 18–21). There is little by way of theological explanation—that came more from Paul in his letter to the church in Corinth, provoked by their abuse of the Lord's Supper (see 1 Corinthians 11:23–34).

Some argue that what was a big meal given a little significance has been turned by the Church into a little meal with lots of significance. That ignores the fact there was already a lot of significance in the simple act of eating a meal together. Fellowship was defined in that way.

Judas was identified as the betrayer at the heart of their shared meal; he could not have offended the norms of loyalty and friendship more completely. It was a similar treason that so outraged Paul: some in Corinth were overeating while others went hungry and 'communion' means 'sharing'.

In Peru, I shared communion in a shanty church on the outskirts of Lima and I recognized that, despite the obvious gulf in terms of culture, those people and I were family together, part of the body of Christ.

Families are blood relatives. God's family members are united by the blood of Jesus, 'poured out for many'. The cup was the sign of a new covenant—a new promise from God that the death of Jesus would be the source of life for the new family.

Reflection

If you share Communion tomorrow, on Maundy Thursday, do as Jesus did and give thanks. Give thanks that his body was broken for you; give thanks that he has brought you into his family, the body of Christ, which is the Church.

SR

115

Not what I will

They went to a place called Gethsemane, and Jesus said to his disciples, 'Sit here while I pray.' He took Peter, James and John along with him, and he began to be deeply distressed and troubled. 'My soul is overwhelmed with sorrow to the point of death,' he said to them. 'Stay here and keep watch.' Going a little farther, he fell to the ground and prayed that if possible the hour might pass from him. 'Abba, Father,' he said, 'everything is possible for you. Take this cup from me. Yet not what I will, but what you will.'

How do you think of Jesus? Kind, gentle, loving, decisive, wise? This is perhaps the one day of the year when we see him, in Mark's words, 'distressed', 'troubled', 'overwhelmed'. His humanity is never more apparent.

You may identify very strongly with this reading. You have longed for human companionship at your moments of greatest stress, but, when you looked for your friends, they weren't there. You have longed for God to intervene and take away the pain—whether physical, emotional or spiritual—and heaven has seemed empty. You have looked for the alternative—the way round rather than the way through—and it hasn't been there.

We read in Hebrews, 'This High Priest of ours understands our weaknesses, for he faced all of the same temptations we do, yet he did not sin' (4:15, NLT). Knowing that, we can be encouraged and strengthened.

Jesus prayed the prayer that we find hardest to pray: 'Not what I will, but what you will.' Most Christians know that submission to God's will is central to walking with him, but most Christians find it incredibly hard to achieve. We prefer the prayer that asks God to do what *we* want, rather than asking him for the strength to do what *he* wants. Thank God that he was in charge at Easter, not me.

Jesus knew that everything was possible for God, but God does not always do everything that is possible.

Reflection

Spend some time keeping watch and praying with Jesus in the Garden of Gethsemane. As Paul puts it, 'I want to know Christ—yes, to know the power of his resurrection and participation in his sufferings, becoming like him in his death...' (Philippians 3:10).

SR

The Son of God forsaken

At three in the afternoon Jesus cried out in a loud voice... 'My God, my God, why have you forsaken me?' When some of those standing near heard this, they said, 'Listen, he's calling Elijah.' Someone ran, filled a sponge with wine vinegar, put it on a staff, and offered it to Jesus to drink. 'Now leave him alone. Let's see if Elijah comes to take him down,' he said. With a loud cry, Jesus breathed his last. The curtain of the temple was torn in two from top to bottom. And when the centurion, who stood there in front of Jesus, saw how he died, he said, 'Surely this man was the Son of God!'

The whole universe shared in the moment of anguish as the Son of God died. The sun was hidden, the earth shook. A cry of anguish, physical and spiritual, echoed into the darkness. The fellowship of the Son with Father, created in eternity, is broken in time and space on that Friday, at 3pm in Jerusalem.

Within seconds, though, the fellowship between human beings and our Creator is repaired. The temple curtain—the massively heavy temple curtain—was torn in two as if it were a piece of paper. There was no longer a barrier; we can know God's presence for ourselves. 'We have confidence,' says the writer to the Hebrews, 'to enter the Most Holy Place by the blood of Jesus, by a new and living way opened for us through the curtain, that is, his body' (10:19–20).

How eloquent is the testimony of the centurion. He had probably been on crucifixion duty many times, yet now he saw something that made him realize Jesus was different. It wasn't obvious to everyone, but he was the closest.

I met Adil in Russia. He was a hard man, a drug addict. He had beaten a man to death. Then he saw Mel Gibson's film *The Passion of the Christ* and realized that Jesus went through all that suffering for him. His life was changed. That's why, despite the horror and sadness in our Bible passage today, it's still called Good Friday.

Reflection

When I survey the wondrous cross
On which the Prince of glory died,
My richest gain I count but loss,
And pour contempt on all my pride.
… Love so amazing, so divine,
Demands my soul, my life, my all.

Isaac Watts (1674–1748)
SR

Doing the right thing

It was Preparation Day (that is, the day before the sabbath). So as evening approached, Joseph of Arimathea, a prominent member of the Council, who was himself waiting for the kingdom of God, went boldly to Pilate and asked for Jesus' body. Pilate was surprised to hear that he was already dead. Summoning the centurion, he asked him if Jesus had already died. When he learned from the centurion that it was so, he gave the body to Joseph. So Joseph bought some linen cloth, took down the body, wrapped it in the linen, and placed it in a tomb cut out of rock. Then he rolled a stone against the entrance of the tomb.

Friday crucifixions were tricky in Israel. If the prisoner wasn't dead before nightfall, the sabbath had arrived and nothing could happen for at least 24 hours, probably 36. Jesus, though, was already dead; there was time to bury him.

His friends had fled. Who could step into the gap? Cue Joseph of Arimathea. He was rich—he had his own tomb ready. He was a well-known man, prominent and influential—a member of the Council. That's the same Council that had made sure Jesus was arrested, sentenced and executed. Can you imagine the gossip, the comments? The risk that Joseph took was social and political: what he did could have ended a man's career or at least his social life. Jesus may have been dead, but he was still a blasphemer, a criminal, an outcast in the eyes of the majority at that time. We don't know whether Joseph

spoke up for Jesus while he was alive, but we do know that he was determined to do the right thing for him now that he was dead, whatever the cost. So the centurion gave a verbal death certificate and Pilate gave permission for the burial. Having dealt with the bureaucracy of the occupying power, Joseph ensured that all was done decently.

Mark wanted to emphasize that Jesus was dead. The Bible offers no assistance to those who want to believe that Jesus was unconscious and revived in the tomb. Joseph was the first to take risks; others were later executed for insisting that Jesus had risen from the dead. How many people do you know who would die to uphold a lie?

Reflection

What risks to our social standing are we prepared to take for Jesus?

SR

MARK 16:1–7 (TNIV, ABRIDGED)

He has risen!

When the sabbath was over, Mary Magdalene, Mary the mother of James, and Salome bought spices so that they might go to anoint Jesus' body. Very early on the first day of the week… they were on their way to the tomb and they asked each other, 'Who will roll the stone away from the entrance of the tomb?' But when they looked up, they saw that the stone, which was very large, had been rolled away. As they entered the tomb, they saw a young man dressed in a white robe… and they were alarmed. 'Don't be alarmed,' he said. 'You are looking for Jesus the Nazarene, who was crucified. He has risen! He is not here… But go, tell his disciples and Peter, "He is going ahead of you into Galilee. There you will see him, just as he told you."'

You can't help but admire these women. In the midst of their own emotional trauma, watching Jesus die in agony and seeking to comfort his mother, they were ready to do what they could and complete the tasks of burial that Joseph had begun.

There was a practical problem: the large stone. Their commitment took them to the tomb all the same, where they discovered that God had been there first. Isn't one of the glories of the Easter story that the women were the first to discover the greatest truth in the history of the world? Perhaps the Church still needs to learn to take women as seriously as God did that first Easter Day.

In a moment, their world had been turned upside down. No wonder they were alarmed! Indeed, the resurrection still alarms people. It alarms the rationalist who does not believe it is possible. It alarms the secularist who would prefer religion to stay inside sealed rooms, not come bursting out. Sadly, at times, it even seems to alarm some parts of the Church.

The joy of Easter came with a command and a promise. The women had seen the empty tomb and now they had to go and share the good news with others. The promise was that Jesus would go before them and they would see him for themselves.

Prayer

Today, Lord, release your resurrection life once again—to me, to your Church, to your needy world. Thank you that, each step I take, you have gone before.

SR

Love God, love people

One of the teachers of the law came and heard them [Jesus and the Sadducees] debating. Noticing that Jesus had given them a good answer, he asked him, 'Of all the commandments, which is the most important?' 'The most important one,' answered Jesus, 'is this: "Hear, O Israel: the Lord our God, the Lord is one. Love the Lord your God with all your heart and with all your soul and with all your mind and with all your strength." The second is this: "Love your neighbour as yourself." There is no commandment greater than these.'

In recording the key conversations between Jesus and his friends—and enemies—as the first Good Friday loomed large, Mark highlighted the universally significant issues in the challenge that the risen Jesus is, and makes, to his audience. He showed that Jesus was assuming divine authority in entering Jerusalem and cleansing the temple. Now he gets right to the heart of God's expectations of us.

It is one thing to say that we should love God, but what do we do because we love God? The Jews had been brilliant at developing their handbook of religious observance. What to wear, what to do and not do on the sabbath, how to make sacrifices at the temple—the list was endless. It was also fatally flawed.

The rulebook had got in the way of caring about people. Religious rituals had become a substitute for God's reality, as the Old Testament prophets had warned. Here's one paraphrase of Isaiah 1:13–15: 'I can't stand your trivial religious games: Monthly conferences, weekly sabbaths, special meetings—meetings, meetings, meetings—I can't stand one more!… I'm sick of your religion, religion, religion, while you go right on sinning. When you put on your next prayer-performance, I'll be looking the other way…' (*The Message*).

It's simple. If God made people in his own image, then how we treat people reflects what we think of God. We cannot love God without loving our neighbours. As the marriage service says, 'What God has joined together, let no one put asunder' and that applies to the two great commandments, too.

Prayer

Dear Lord, help me to see you in all the people I meet, and love and serve them as if I was loving and serving you.

SR

The promise of persecution

'You must be on your guard. You will be handed over to the local councils and flogged in the synagogues. On account of me you will stand before governors and kings as witnesses to them. And the gospel must first be preached to all nations. Whenever you are arrested and brought to trial, do not worry beforehand about what to say. Just say whatever is given you at the time, for it is not you speaking, but the Holy Spirit.'

Jesus said these words to his disciples before his own trial and execution, but they were also a promise of what would happen after his resurrection. The disciples might have been forgiven for thinking that the triumph of Easter Day would make all that irrelevant. No: Easter Day offers a vital perspective on Christian suffering, but not a bypass.

Not so long ago, I visited Russia, where I met a Christian who risks his life to keep in touch with and encourage the isolated handful of believers in Chechnya, sharing the good news of Jesus whenever he can. 'I speak to Muslims,' said Peter. 'They know there are Muslims who are willing to die for their faith. If I am not willing to die for my faith, I lose all credibility.'

Jesus was determined that faith should be rooted in reality. That reality was painful—but also productive. Believers would stand before those with power and those with power would discover that they could not crush people who refused to acknowledge their authority.

Nero actually forced out Christians from across the Roman empire. Eventually that empire became Christian. Modern China attempted to destroy the church, and is now home to the largest Christian community on the planet: 60–80 million and growing. The blood of the martyrs has indeed been the seed of the Church.

While writing these notes, I met a Turkish Christian. He was on trial, facing up to nine years in prison for 'insulting Turkishness'. When the prosecutor reminded him that he could be sent to prison, he replied that he would start a church in the prison. I suspect that today's passage became true once again in that courtroom.

Reflection

Jesus promised two things to his disciples: persecution and his presence through the gift of the Holy Spirit.

SR

On guard!

'But about that day or hour no one knows, not even the angels in heaven, nor the Son, but only the Father. Be on guard! Be alert! You do not know when that time will come. It's like a man going away: He leaves his house and puts his servants in charge, each with an assigned task, and tells the one at the door to keep watch. Therefore keep watch because you do not know when the owner of the house will come back—whether in the evening, or at midnight, or when the cock crows, or at dawn. If he comes suddenly, do not let him find you sleeping. What I say to you, I say to everyone: "Watch!"'

Before Jesus left his disciples, he promised to return, along with a very specific command: 'Be on guard! Be alert! Watch!' He echoed the very request he made of his three closest friends in Gethsemane (14:34), who, in a spectacularly quiet way, failed him completely.

For 2000 years you would have thought the command was, 'Work out the date! Spend years on the calculations! If you get it wrong, try again!' Every generation has seen some Christians convinced that they are part of the final generation. Each successive disappointment lessens the faith of others that Jesus will return at all.

Jesus was emphatic: even he did not know the time or the date. However, he was equally emphatic that his Father did and would keep his promise. That's why the command was to be 'on guard'.

Every schoolchild understands the problem. The teacher sets the task, then leaves the room, telling the children to continue with their work. Some relax, thinking that there will be enough time if they get started in a while. Then the teacher returns suddenly and some are caught out, being idle rather than busy.

Of course Jesus is more than a teacher figure, but he knows the human failing of always assuming that there is enough time, that the important things can wait until tomorrow. Serving God is not a homework chore; it is the purpose of living and the source of joyful fulfilment. Don't put off until tomorrow what you will most enjoy doing today!

Prayer

Lord, keep us alert to all the possibilities of joyful service as we look for your return. Amen

SR

Always with you

While he was in Bethany, reclining at the table in the home of Simon the Leper, a woman came with an alabaster jar of very expensive perfume, made of pure nard. She broke the jar and poured the perfume on his head. Some of those present were saying indignantly to one another, 'Why this waste of perfume? It could have been sold for more than a year's wages and the money given to the poor.' And they rebuked her harshly. 'Leave her alone,' said Jesus. 'Why are you bothering her? She has done a beautiful thing to me. The poor you will always have with you, and you can help them any time you want. But you will not always have me. She did what she could. She poured perfume on my body beforehand to prepare for my burial.'

We see Jesus and his friends relaxing around the table, an oasis of peace in a frenetic week. Then, controversy: a woman enters and anoints Jesus with an expensive and powerful perfume. As the air becomes heavy with its scent, the conversation becomes heated.

It is difficult for us to understand the nuances of the situation. We know that, at feasts, the honoured guests might be anointed: 'You prepare a table before me in the presence of my enemies. You anoint my head with oil…' (Psalm 23:5) Also, it was the custom to make a special gift to the poor on the evening before Passover. Why, then, did the guests react so sharply in this case? Were they embarrassed and offended by the woman's public display of devotion?

I heard a minister use this passage to encourage people to give to a church building programme, arguing that our devotion to Jesus is best expressed by investing in a place of worship, not helping the poor. I don't think that was what Jesus meant! He quoted Deuteronomy 15:11—'There will always be poor people in the land'—a verse that continues by commanding our generosity to such people.

What Jesus says in this passage is not a get-out clause, but reinforcement. His kind words about the woman indicated that her action was appreciated and that, in his absence, we can express our devotion to him through our care for the needy (Proverbs 14:31).

Reflection
'Whatever you did for one of the least of these… you did for me'
(Matthew 25:40).

SR

I don't believe it!

When Jesus rose early on the first day of the week, he appeared first to Mary Magdalene, out of whom he had driven seven demons. She went and told those who had been with him and who were mourning and weeping. When they heard that Jesus was alive… they did not believe it. Afterwards Jesus appeared in a different form to two of them while they were walking in the country. These returned and reported it to the rest; but they did not believe them either. Later Jesus appeared to the Eleven as they were eating; he rebuked them for their lack of faith and their stubborn refusal to believe those who had seen him after he had risen.

Most scholars agree that the last eleven verses of Mark are almost certainly added by a later writer in the absence of Mark's intended conclusion. Otherwise, the Gospel would finish with women trembling, bewildered, silent and afraid (see 16:8)! However, these verses are still well worth reading as a kind of early Church summary of what was the end of the beginning.

Can you blame those who refused to believe Mary's resurrection testimony? For centuries people have struggled to believe it. Paul, however, was clear that this is the core belief of Christianity: 'If Christ has not been raised, our preaching is useless and so is your faith' (1 Corinthians 15:14). For me, it worked the other way. At university, I was ready to ditch my Christian upbringing, but I was studying history and I couldn't escape the historical evidence for the resurrec-

tion. If that was true, then so was the rest.

When you do believe, faith reveals the risen Christ in all sorts of places. I've seen him in people dedicated to transforming their community in his name; I've seen him reflected in the devoted eyes of a woman in Chechnya who had been threatened with crucifixion when she told her work colleagues that she was a Christian.

Mark simply records that Mary and the disciples saw Jesus with their own eyes. Either it was true or they were liars who based the rest of their lives on that lie. If you've met with him, then you know he's alive, whatever anyone else may say.

Prayer

Dear Lord, on the days we doubt, come to us again as gently as you appeared to Mary. Amen

SR

124

Famous last words

He [Jesus] said to them, 'Go into all the world and preach the gospel to all creation. Whoever believes and is baptized will be saved, but whoever does not believe will be condemned. And these signs will accompany those who believe: in my name they will drive out demons; they will speak in new tongues; they will pick up snakes with their hands; and when they drink deadly poison, it will not hurt them at all; they will place their hands on people who are ill, and they will get well.' After the Lord Jesus had spoken to them, he was taken up into heaven and he sat at the right hand of God. Then the disciples went out and preached everywhere, and the Lord worked with them and confirmed his word by the signs that accompanied it.

In these final few verses, we have Jesus' last words and a rapid summary of what happened next. There are four key points.

First, the disciples were given a task. The learners were now missionaries. Everything that they had absorbed from Jesus was to be articulated and lived out—it was truly universal, for the whole world and the whole creation.

Second, the gospel was only good news to those who received it—Jesus speaks of condemnation for those who choose not to believe. That can be hard to accept—can't everyone believe what they like? Of course they can. Religious freedom is a vital aspect of human rights, but that does not oblige us to hold all beliefs as equally true. Christianity insists that Jesus is the way, the truth and the life (John 14:6). Of course, this must be proclaimed with sensitivity and love and lived out with passion and compassion, but it must never be compromised.

Third, the strange words about snakes and poison indicate a general principle: when God is at work, miracles happen. Now, as then, these are signs of God's kingdom, glimpses of what is to come—no demons, no pain, no tears, no death.

Finally, the joy, the privilege and the blessing of being a Christian is that working *for* God is all about working *with* God. As Paul wrote, 'we are God's co-workers' (1 Corinthians 3:9). How exciting is that?

Prayer

Lord, help me to see the signs of you at work—in me and through me.
Amen

SR

Faith under fire

The idea of 'being a martyr' has tended to be limited to stories of long ago that we might hear in church or at school, or else the phrase is used to describe somebody who is 'a martyr to their corns' or 'enjoys being a bit of a martyr'. In other words, they like to moan.

More recently, and tragically, we have become familiar with a quite different form of martyrdom—that of the suicide bomber who chooses to kill him- or herself together with a lot of innocent people for the sake of a political or religious goal. Martyrdom as an act of violence is quite alien to the traditional—and also biblical—idea of a martyr as somebody who is prepared to sacrifice themselves for the sake of their beliefs. The concept is quintessentially that of being a victim, not in any way an aggressor.

Far from involving any kind of 'heroic' posturing, martyrdom in the past has involved a death that has often been humiliating and not self-inflicted but subject to the whims of the executioners. Think of Alphege (whom we will meet in these readings), beaten to death with ox bones by a drunken mob; the South Pacific missionary James Chalmers (remembered by the Anglican calendar on 2 September),

beheaded, cooked with sago and then eaten; think, above all, of Jesus, who was publicly flogged and then crucified—the most shameful death possible at that time and in that culture.

Over the next week or so, we will consider three other Christian martyrs besides Alphege—namely, Mark (the Gospel writer), George (patron saint of England) and Pierre Chanel, a 19th-century Catholic priest and missionary. Theirs are very different stories—some well-documented, others tinged with legend—but all sharing similar themes of courage, endurance and faithful witness.

As we read, we may find their stories inspiring, moving us to dream of standing up for our own faith in desperate times. We may, on the other hand, feel that we are the least heroic person we know, highly likely to crumple under any form of duress. In fact, the Bible passages that we shall study in the coming days offer encouragement even for the most timid of heart. Remember: God has a history of using the most unlikely people to do the most amazing works and his definition of a hero is very different from that of this world.

Naomi Starkey

MATTHEW 16:24–26 (TNIV)

Steadfast leadership

Then Jesus said to his disciples, 'Whoever wants to be my disciple must deny themselves and take up their cross and follow me. For whoever wants to save their life will lose it, but whoever loses their life for me will find it. What good will it be for you to gain the whole world, yet forfeit your soul? Or what can you give in exchange for your soul?'

This is the day in the Anglican calendar when Alphege is remembered—the then Archbishop of Canterbury, martyred in 1012. He was murdered in Greenwich, now a chic part of south-east London, but then simply a settlement along the Thames where the invading Danes moored their longboats. That turbulent era is graphically described in *The Anglo-Saxon Chronicle*, the historical record begun in King Alfred's reign.

Alphege was captured during the sack of Canterbury in 1011, imprisoned for seven months and then murdered after he advised against paying the enormous ransom demanded for his safe release. He died at the hands of the occupying army, wielding grotesque 'weapons', although some said that a final blow with an axe was an act of mercy by one of the Danes, who had come to faith through Alphege's witness. The traditional site of his martyrdom is marked by St Alfege (an alternative spelling of his name) Church, the present building being the third since his death.

The daunting challenge issued by Jesus in today's passage—'whoever loses his life for me will find it'—is exemplified in Alphege's life and death. Given his role as Archbishop, he was urged to flee to safety but chose instead to stay with the helpless local people and face the invaders together with them.

We may be tempted to focus on the horror of losing our lives, but we should remember that Jesus' words are actually a promise: if we cling to what we fear to lose, we will lose it anyway. If we give ourselves freely into Jesus' hands, he will bless us with the life of the Spirit that is abundant and eternal.

Prayer

Lord God, we thank you for the example of Alphege. May we honour his memory and learn lessons from his courageous life for our own journey of faith.

NS

Peace in the storm

Lord, how many are my foes! How many rise up against me! Many are saying of me, 'God will not deliver him.' But you, Lord, are a shield around me, my glory, the one who lifts my head high. I call out to the Lord, and he answers me from his holy mountain. I lie down and sleep; I wake again, because the Lord sustains me. I will not fear though tens of thousands assail me on every side. Arise, Lord! Deliver me, my God! Strike all my enemies on the jaw; break the teeth of the wicked. From the Lord comes deliverance. May your blessing be on your people.

This is an example of one of those psalms that has some lovely verses and then lets rip with a no holds barred onslaught, which sounds most unbiblical to our modern ears. Not content with simply lamenting the number of his enemies, the psalmist calls on God to attack them on his behalf.

Trusting in God's protection does not mean that we do not feel anger and aggression towards those who are making life hard for us. The character of Gene Hunt in BBC TV's *Life on Mars*—an unreconstructed 1970s macho cop—is hardly a model of Christian behaviour, yet he often used violence to sort out a situation not because he loved violence, but because he hated crime and what it did to his beloved city of Manchester.

The Anglo-Saxon Chronicle does not tell us whether Alphege maintained his composure throughout his seven months of imprison-

ment, although, as mentioned yesterday, there is the tradition that he managed to share the gospel with one of his captors. Despite his impending fate, he remained true to the imperative to spread the good news of Jesus. It may well have been that the astonishing verses about 'I lie down and sleep; I wake again, because the Lord sustains me' could have held true for him. Even in the most gruelling of circumstances, he could find peace and rest in the presence of his Lord, whether or not he privately raged at the horrors being perpetrated in his country.

Prayer

Pray for times of peace and rest for those who have to endure anarchy and danger in places such as Somalia, the Democratic Republic of the Congo and Darfur.

NS

At the darkest hour

But now, this is what the Lord says…: 'Do not fear, for I have redeemed you; I have summoned you by name; you are mine. When you pass through the waters, I will be with you; and when you pass through the rivers, they will not sweep over you. When you walk through the fire, you will not be burned… For I am the Lord your God, the Holy One of Israel, your Saviour… I will bring your children from the east and gather you from the west. I will say to the north, 'Give them up!' and to the south, 'Do not hold them back.' Bring my sons from afar and my daughters from the ends of the earth—everyone who is called by my name, whom I created for my glory, whom I formed and made.'

The fire, flood and exile described by the Bible passage would have been experiences all too common in Alphege's lifetime, and for hundreds of years before and after. Back in 793, *The Anglo-Saxon Chronicle* spoke of 'dragons' (an interesting link to our George readings!) in the sky, terrible storms, famine and then slaughter in Lindisfarne by invaders from across the sea.

The scholar Alcuin of York (c.735–804) wrote that the Viking invasions were God's punishment for sinfulness, quoting Jeremiah 1:14: 'The Lord said to me, "From the north disaster will be poured out on all who live in the land".' While we may dispute Alcuin's perspective, Old Testament prophets such as Isaiah declared that the people of Israel were punished by exile because they refused to keep the terms of God's covenant.

What we read in today's passage, however, is that, despite the hard times, God promises to restore his people's fortunes. He may punish, but then he forgives—like any parent. Even in the darkest hour, his presence is with them—and not just with the faithful few but all his children, even those who have continued in disobedience.

We may suffer through no fault of our own, caught up in events resulting from other people's wrong decisions and sinful motives, but we have here our Father's reassurance that he continues to hold on to us and even on to those whose selfish impulses are wreaking havoc all around them.

Reflection

'Do not be afraid, for I am with you'
(Isaiah 43:5).

NS

Soldier in the army of the Lord

Finally, be strong in the Lord and in his mighty power. Put on the full armour of God, so that you can take your stand against the devil's schemes. For our struggle is not against flesh and blood, but... against the authorities, against the powers of this dark world and against the spiritual forces of evil in the heavenly realms. Therefore put on the full armour of God, so that when the day of evil comes, you may be able to stand your ground... And pray in the Spirit on all occasions with all kinds of prayers and requests... Pray also for me, that whenever I speak, words may be given me so that I will fearlessly make known the mystery of the gospel, for which I am an ambassador in chains.

Our next martyr is George—an extraordinarily popular saint, particularly in the Eastern Church, considering how little is known about him. He is patron saint of not only England but also Canada, Ethiopia, Greece, Georgia and many other places and groups. Even if historical facts about his life are thin on the ground, his story has inspired generations and his flag continues to be flown whenever the England football team has another go at winning an international trophy.

The convention is that George was born in third-century Cappadocia (part of modern-day Turkey) to Christian parents but grew up in Palestine, where he joined the Roman army. When the emperor Diocletian began persecuting believers, George resigned from his military post in protest. He was eventually arrested, gruesomely tortured and executed.

The passage in Ephesians from which our reading is taken gives a precise inventory of a Roman soldier's kit—presumably something with which George would have been familiar. Each part is here linked to some aspect of Christian discipleship. As the soldier is prepared for battle, so should we be ready for 'the day of evil' that will surely come.

We may not warm to military imagery, but we can still hear the message: be prayerful, be prepared. We are not called to go out and pick fights to defend our beliefs, but, like George, we should be ready to hold our ground if and when it becomes necessary.

Prayer

Lord God, when the time comes, please give us the strength we need to take the stand that we must.

NS

REVELATION 12:7–12 (TNIV, ABRIDGED)

Fighting the dragon

And there was war in heaven. Michael and his angels fought against the dragon, and the dragon and his angels fought back. But he was not strong enough, and they lost their place in heaven. The great dragon was hurled down—that ancient snake called the devil... Then I heard a loud voice in heaven say: 'Now have come the salvation and the power and the kingdom of our God, and the authority of his Messiah. For the accuser of our brothers and sisters... has been hurled down. They triumphed over him by the blood of the Lamb and by the word of their testimony; they did not love their lives so much as to shrink from death. Therefore... woe to the earth and the sea, because the devil has gone down to you! He is filled with fury, because he knows that his time is short.'

George is best known for his legendary dragon-slaying. The story was first widely circulated in a 15th-century book, *The Golden Legend*. It presents a familiar series of events: hero comes to city besieged by monster, princess is next victim, hero deals with monster and saves princess. Rather than the usual 'hero marries princess' ending, however, George arranges for the baptism of the king and his people and builds a church where a healing spring then appears.

Our Bible passage speaks of war in heaven, angels fighting Satan, the 'ancient snake', in a scene that is even more dramatic than the story of George. It uses vivid poetic language to demonstrate the victory of the kingdom of heaven over the forces of darkness.

What can we learn from all this? First, that the battle against evil is not a question of equally balanced forces, the final outcome doubtful, as it has already been won on the cross when Christ willingly gave his life to redeem us. Second, as in the legend of George, we may be called to 'slay a dragon'. There may be a battle that we are called to fight, a difficult task that we are given to do, and we can do it in the confidence that, if God has called us, he will give us the strength we need.

Reflection

'The Lord will rescue me from every evil attack and will bring me safely to his heavenly kingdom'
(2 Timothy 4:18).

NS

Just doing his job

Remember Jesus Christ, raised from the dead, descended from David. This is my gospel, for which I am suffering even to the point of being chained like a criminal. But God's word is not chained. Therefore I endure everything for the sake of the elect, that they too may obtain the salvation that is in Christ Jesus, with eternal glory. Here is a trustworthy saying: If we died with him, we will also live with him; if we endure, we will also reign with him.

What's the significance of George for us today? There are occasional campaigns to replace him as England's patron saint with one more historical and relevant to this country. If we set aside the romantic dragon-slaying, though, we can see that George's story does have a lesson for us. It is an example of an ordinary man refusing to renounce what he knows to be true, even if it means disgrace and death.

It is interesting how often people say, 'I'm not a hero—I was just doing my job' when they have carried out some exemplary act of bravery. While a conventional Hollywood hero can usually be identified by the far-off look in his eyes and his finely toned physique, real-life heroes are very like us. What marks them out is their willingness to take personal risks for the sake of a greater good. Paul Rusesagabina is one such person. His story is told in the film *Hotel Rwanda*, which shows how he used his position as a hotel manager to save more than 1000 refugees during the 1994 genocide.

Paul, writing to his protégé Timothy, describes how he is 'just doing his job'. Jesus called him to spread the good news to the nations and he was just continuing that work, even though he was in chains and faced possible execution. He believed that bringing salvation to others was worth all the suffering and humiliation heaped on him.

We may be lucky enough never to have to face such challenging circumstances, but we can pray for the strengthening of our own faith, so that we understand it for the amazing gift that it is and feel confident enough in what we believe to share it sensitively with others.

Prayer

Father God, give us grace to do the work that you have given us—the task of spreading your message of salvation—no matter what the cost to ourselves.

NS

Strengthened by the Spirit

Jesus said to them: 'Watch out that no one deceives you. Many will come in my name, claiming, "I am he", and will deceive many. When you hear of wars and rumours of wars, do not be alarmed. Such things must happen, but the end is still to come... You will be handed over to the local councils and flogged in the synagogues. On account of me you will stand before governors and kings as witnesses to them. And the gospel must first be preached to all nations. Whenever you are arrested and brought to trial, do not worry beforehand about what to say. Just say whatever is given you at the time, for it is not you speaking, but the Holy Spirit.'

For churches that follow the lectionary—a pattern of Bible readings linked to the Church calendar—the designated Gospel for this day is Mark. Mark's Gospel is short, lively and was probably the first to be written—the traditional view is that it was based largely on the preaching of Peter. The author was also known as John Mark and he appears several times in Acts, as well as in Paul's letters.

The rest of Mark's story is more speculative. He is believed to have founded the church in Africa by establishing the faith in Alexandria, from where it spread throughout Egypt and beyond. He was martyred in Alexandria in AD67, tied to horses and dragged through the streets until he died from his injuries.

Our Bible passage comes from a section of Mark's Gospel known as the 'Little Apocalypse', where Jesus warns of the troubles to come—specifically, the persecution his followers will face as they spread the gospel. His words would have sounded as daunting to his original audience as they do to us as they were mostly law-abiding, devout Jewish believers, who would hardly expect to find themselves being 'flogged in the synagogues'.

Once again, however, we hear the reassurance that we are not alone. Even if we are called to justify what we believe to the most unsympathetic of hearers, we need not fear because the Holy Spirit will give us the words we need.

Reflection

Jesus also warns about the danger of deception. As we grow in faith, it is important that we learn more about what Christians believe and why, so that we can discern true teaching from false.

NS

A second chance

Some time later Paul said to Barnabas, 'Let us go back and visit the believers in all the towns where we preached the word of the Lord and see how they are doing.' Barnabas wanted to take John, also called Mark, with them, but Paul did not think it wise to take him, because he had deserted them in Pamphylia and had not continued with them in the work. They had such a sharp disagreement that they parted company. Barnabas took Mark and sailed for Cyprus, but Paul chose Silas and left, commended by the believers to the grace of the Lord.

This is probably the best-known of Mark's appearances in the book of Acts and it is not an auspicious one. He first joined up with Paul and Barnabas (who was his cousin) when he accompanied them from Jerusalem back to the recently founded church in Antioch (Acts 12:25). He was listed as their 'helper' (13:5) on Paul's first missionary journey in Asia Minor (modern Turkey), but for some reason he dropped out along the way and returned to Jerusalem.

When Barnabas wanted Mark to accompany them on a second journey, Paul's refusal led to a 'sharp disagreement' and a breakdown in what had been an extremely fruitful working relationship. We hear no more of Mark in Acts, but, from the warmth with which Paul later mentions him (see especially 2 Timothy 4:11), it is clear that they were eventually reconciled.

It is salutary to see that bickering and falling out are not new phenomena in Christian circles, nor are disputes about personnel. Paul's judgment regarding Mark may have seemed right at the time, but, in the longer term, Mark's suitability for the great task of spreading the gospel was clearly in no doubt at all.

We may feel that we once made a mistake that has blighted later opportunities, even cast a shadow over the rest of our lives. Thank God that, if we come to him, he is always ready to forgive our errors and give us a new start. Other people may judge us as lacking in ability, but, if God calls us, he will equip us for the task.

Reflection

'He who began a good work in you will carry it on to completion until the day of Christ Jesus' (Philippians 1:6).

NS

Growing up in Christ

Christ himself gave the apostles, the prophets, the evangelists, the pastors and teachers, to equip his people for works of service, so that the body of Christ may be built up until we all reach unity in the faith and in the knowledge of the Son of God and become mature, attaining to the whole measure of the fullness of Christ. Then we will no longer be infants, tossed back and forth by the waves, and blown here and there by every wind of teaching and by the cunning and craftiness of people in their deceitful scheming. Instead, speaking the truth in love, we will in all things grow up into him who is the head, that is, Christ.

Another of the traditions associated with Mark (though not explicit in the New Testament) is that he was one of those who ran away when Jesus was arrested in Gethsemane: 'A young man, wearing nothing but a linen garment, was following Jesus. When they [the crowd] seized him, he fled naked, leaving his garment behind' (Mark 14:51–52). He was just as terrified as Jesus' other followers, a dropout from his first missionary journey, notable for his youth—how ironic that the artistic symbol associated with Mark is a lion, synonymous with bravery.

What a relief, then, that our Bible reading reinforces the message that, while we may now be like tiny babies in faith terms, with God's help we can grow as Christians. In today's 'instant gratification' culture, it is easy to forget the importance of taking time, learning on the job, doing better the next time. God wants real maturity, seasoned believers, 'to equip his people for works of service', not just a handful of spiritual prodigies, who may look and sound good but then crash and burn.

Note the phrase 'speaking the truth in love'—a frequently abused phrase that can end up meaning 'speaking severely to another Christian while smiling at them'. It is worth remembering the context here: we speak the truth lovingly so that 'we will in all things grow up into him [Christ]', not so that we can be hypercritical under the guise of 'helping'.

Prayer

Thank you, heavenly Father, that we are your sons and daughters. May we grow in the light of your love until we reach true maturity, even the fullness of your son and our brother, Jesus.

NS

Sent to all the nations

Then the eleven disciples went to Galilee, to the mountain where Jesus had told them to go. When they saw him, they worshipped him; but some doubted. Then Jesus came to them and said, 'All authority in heaven and on earth has been given to me. Therefore go and make disciples of all nations, baptizing them in the name of the Father and of the Son and of the Holy Spirit, and teaching them to obey everything I have commanded you. And surely I am with you always, to the very end of the age.'

Compared with Mark the evangelist, George the dragon-slayer or even Archbishop Alphege, the name of Pierre (or Peter) Chanel will be known to relatively few, yet this Catholic priest is commemorated today because of his martyrdom in the South Pacific.

Born in France, Chanel was ordained in his mid-20s and, in 1836, set off to the far side of the world. He eventually arrived at Futuna Island, in what was then known as the New Hebrides, and was clubbed to death there on 28 April 1841 on the orders of the king, who resented the coming of Christianity. The island was so remote that news of Chanel's death took nearly a year to get to France. He had truly gone to the ends of the earth to help make disciples.

Many people—even Christians— feel uncomfortable with the idea of 'missionary work', associating it with cultural insensitivity and heavy-handed colonialism. Yet, mission is what Jesus commanded his followers to do. Since then, the good news has spread from nation to nation and, today, ironically, Christianity is generally stronger in the developing world than in the nations who sent out so many missionaries.

It is strangely reassuring to read that, even as the Eleven met the risen Jesus face to face for the last time, some of them still 'doubted'. They had also heard and seen the words, miracles, parables, resurrection. To them—and us and all toiling at the coal-face of mission today, tempted to despair at superficial responses and infinitesimally slow progress—Jesus promises his presence, now and always.

Prayer

Thank you, Jesus, that you know some of us still doubt, despite everything you have done for us. Help us in our unbelief.

NS

Pass it on

Keep your head in all situations, endure hardship, do the work of an evangelist, discharge all the duties of your ministry. For I am already being poured out like a drink offering, and the time for my departure is near. I have fought the good fight, I have finished the race, I have kept the faith. Now there is in store for me the crown of righteousness, which the Lord, the righteous Judge, will award to me on that day—and not only to me, but also to all who have longed for his appearing.

The apostle Paul wrote these moving words to Timothy as he knew that his own ministry was drawing to a close. He was imprisoned in Rome, probably chained in a damp dungeon (1:16), and knew that he had to hand on his work, even though it was very far from finished (4:13).

Pierre Chanel, like so many missionaries before and after, was taken from his task before he had time to secure the spiritual foundations that he had laid. Other events, sometimes less calamitous but still difficult, can have a similar result, such as ill health, a collapse in local relationships, war, shortage of funds—these are all ways in which a calling can be cut short, the worker returned home bewildered, even disillusioned.

We may find ourselves having to leave a job that we know is only just beginning. Our hearts may churn with a mixture of wounded pride, anxiety and downright irritation—we are not ready to go yet! We should note, then, that Paul's words (which on first reading can sound self-centred), in fact simply emphasize how he realizes that his part of the work is done. It will go on, however, as Timothy and others like him 'do the work of an evangelist' and 'discharge all the duties of [their] ministry'. Like Paul, we have to accept when it is time for another to take over. It is in God's hands and he will ensure that it continues.

Just a few months after Chanel's death, it is recorded that all the islanders became Christians and today Futuna Island is still noted for the devout Catholicism of its inhabitants.

Reflection

Though we may feel that we are being 'poured out like a drink offering', we too have the hope of a 'crown of righteousness'.

NS

The day of the Lord

When [the Lamb] opened the fifth seal, I saw... the souls of those who had been slain because of the word of God and the testimony they had maintained. They called out in a loud voice, 'How long, Sovereign Lord, holy and true, until you judge the inhabitants of the earth and avenge our blood?' Then each of them was given a white robe, and they were told to wait a little longer... I watched as he opened the sixth seal. There was a great earthquake. The sun turned black... the whole moon turned blood red, and the stars in the sky fell to earth... The sky receded like a scroll, rolling up, and every mountain and island was removed from its place.

In the apocalyptic, picture code language of Revelation, we are told of a time when God will act decisively to draw history to a close. A time will come when the work of the evangelists will be over and the witness of the martyrs completed. The old order will pass away and the Creator will make the world new again.

Like the voices of the martyrs crying out to God for vindication, we may want to ask, 'How long, Sovereign Lord?' How long before his purposes behind what has happened in our lives, in our communities, our nations are finally revealed? If we have personally made sacrifices of friendships, wider family ties, community, career advancement or health in obedience to God's calling, we may long to know that it has been worth it.

We are reminded here that there is a wider dimension to life than we can glimpse from our own mortal perspective. The temptation is to feel that we are insignificant, our decisions and actions of no account in the great scheme of things, but, in fact, we cannot begin to see the full significance of our actions, the consequences of our relationships with others. One day, though, all will be made clear.

Reflection

'The throne of God and of the Lamb will be in the city, and his servants will serve him. They will see his face, and his name will be on their foreheads... They will not need the light of a lamp or the light of the sun, for the Lord God will give them light. And they will reign for ever and ever' (Revelation 22:3–5).

NS

The BRF
Magazine

Richard Fisher writes...

A 'fellowship' is a group of people who come together to share a particular aim or interest, who take pleasure in each other's company and in the goals they have in common. At BRF, the Bible Reading Fellowship, we are well aware of the benefits of this sharing, as the staff team works together to produce Bible reading notes and books, and as the Barnabas ministry team pool their creativity and expertise to inspire the pupils, teachers and children's workers they meet through the year.

We also know how encouraging it is to have other people around us to share our spiritual journey. So in this issue of the BRF Magazine, Ceri Ellis, who is part of our Marketing team, sets out the advantages of reading regularly as a group of subscribers, while Tony Horsfall writes on his work as a mentor and retreat leader, accompanying others in their walk with God.

One central aspect of fellowship is sharing meals together, and two of our contributors in this issue take food as their theme. First comes an extract from this year's Lent book, *Fasting and Feasting* by Gordon Giles, and then Margaret Withers writes about how to involve the whole congregation in Holy Communion, the meal that defines our fellowship with Jesus Christ and with other believers.

Within those congregations, children are an important but often neglected part of our fellow-ship. At BRF we have a burgeoning ministry among children, and Jane Butcher, the *Barnabas* team member based in the Midlands, explains part of her role, bringing the Bible alive in schools. We would be delighted if you were inspired by her report to join in the work in whatever way you can.

Finally, *New Daylight* editor Naomi Starkey reminds us that our discipleship involves, first and foremost, drawing closer to God, who is active in the world of human beings and loves to work in fellowship with us. Naomi recommends two BRF books that encourage us to collaborate with God and other people in the work to which he calls us.

Thank you for your continued prayers for BRF. We very much appreciate your 'partnership in the gospel' (Philippians 1:5).

Richard Fisher, Chief Executive

Sharing in the Bible together

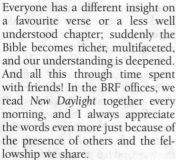

Ceri Ellis

Some people prefer to read the Bible as a solitary act, soaking in that knowledge and wisdom with no interruptions and no outside voices. That's not a bad thing: it's often useful to have time to yourself, studying his word. But there is just as much to gain from joining others to learn all sorts of things we might never have discovered alone.

Everyone has a different insight on a favourite verse or a less well understood chapter; suddenly the Bible becomes richer, multifaceted, and our understanding is deepened. And all this through time spent with friends! In the BRF offices, we read *New Daylight* together every morning, and I always appreciate the words even more just because of the presence of others and the fellowship we share.

At BRF, we are keen to encourage you to spend more time with the Bible and with each other. The group subscription system is a great way to do that. By gathering a minimum of five people subscribing to a mix of any of our Bible reading notes (*New Daylight*, *Guidelines* and *Day by Day with God*) or our prayer and spirituality journal *Quiet Spaces*, you can be classified as a group. What's so great about being in a group? Not only do you get the chance to experience the Bible with your fellow churchgoers or cell group, but you also qualify for a discount on the individual subscription rate, as you do not have to pay postage. With a rolling subscription system, you won't have to renew anything with us: just let us know if you want to change the number of copies you receive.

You'll be pleasantly surprised at the difference four extra heads make when looking at a particular Bible passage. So why not give the groups system a try? Perhaps it will enrich your spiritual life; perhaps it will strengthen your relationships with the people around you. It may even do both! If you would like to start a group in your local area, please phone me on 01865 319709 or email ceri.ellis@brf.org.uk, and I will be happy to start you off on the process.

To compare our individual and group subscription rates, see page 157.

The Editor recommends

Naomi Starkey

The path of Christian discipleship involves both learning more about God—drawing closer to him—and learning more about how we witness in today's culture to what we believe. We can only truly share what we know ourselves, what we can prove from our own experience. A second-hand faith can all too easily end up being no faith at all.

Two recent books published by BRF, *Into Your Hands* and *Growing Women Leaders*, present contrasting and at the same time complementary perspectives on these issues. Both combine an emphasis on knowing what we believe and why with the importance of expressing our beliefs clearly to the watching world.

Kevin Scully's *Into Your Hands* explores what it means to say that God is at work in the world today—specifically, how the hand of God can interact with the actions of human beings, who are themselves acting as 'God's hands' as they go about their daily lives. Beginning with creation and moving on to reflect on the person and work of Jesus, the book considers how God—Father, Son, Spirit—has worked and continues to work to shape the events of history. It also considers how individuals, communities and churches might respond. The concluding section focuses on the events of Jesus' death and resurrection, his broken hands outstretched to bring healing and salvation, as the mystery of redemption unfolds.

Each chapter concludes with questions for discussion or individual reflection, meditative exercises and a prayer. In a foreword warmly endorsing the book, John Sentamu, Archbishop of York, writes, '*Into Your Hands* points to the way God has given us life in his created order and new life in Jesus. It also reminds us that there is a practical working out of our faith. We cannot but want to put our hands on the plough. After all, the future is in our hands as God's invited guests and friends.'

Author Kevin Scully has also written *Sensing the Passion* and *Women on the Way* (both published by Triangle/SPCK), as well as contributing to a number of other books. Ordained in the Church of England, he has served his entire ministry in inner-city London and is currently the rector of St Matthew's, Bethnal Green, in the East End. A former actor and journalist, he has also written ten produced stage works and two radio plays.

By contrast, *Growing Women Leaders* examines a specific issue in the life of the Church (and, by extension, in society in general). As the title states, this is a book about women's leadership in the Church, considering the current situation and looking to the future.

As the years have passed since the Church of England decided to ordain women to the priesthood, it is tempting to assume that the debate on whether women should lead at all is now over. Author Rosie Ward shows, however, that there is still more to do for churches to become places where women and men can truly share authority and have the same opportunities to exercise a ministry of leadership.

This is not just a matter of church policy but of discipleship. Rosie Ward surveys the latest scholarship on key scripture passages relating to women leaders, outlines the long history of women in church leadership, and offers much practical advice on helping women grow as leaders. While avoiding stereotypes, she argues that women have unique gifts to bring to leadership and that they need targeted help to nurture these gifts. If the Church does not utilize women in leadership, not only is their poten-

tial untapped but everybody is impoverished.

The book is written to inspire and nurture women already in leadership, as well as encouraging those exploring a call to this ministry. It is also essential reading for men—all those who work alongside women leaders in the Church and those involved in the selection and training of women for ministry.

Rosie Ward works with the Church Pastoral Aid Society (CPAS), with a particular brief for developing women as leaders in the Church. She is also involved with CPAS's vocations work, encouraging people to consider church ministry. She previously spent eleven years in parish ministry herself, has written *Liberating Women for the Gospel* and three Grove booklets, and has also contributed to *The Church of England Newspaper*, *Ministry Today*, *Women Alive* and *Anvil*.

In Hebrews 13, we find a prayer for all believers, that 'the God of peace [may]… equip you with everything good for doing his will' (vv. 20–21, TNIV). As we grow in stature as disciples, we will find ourselves equipped for the tasks to which God calls us in his world. It is my prayer that these two books, in their different ways, will provide help in this process for all who read them.

To order a copy of Into Your Hands or Growing Women Leaders, *please turn to the order form on page 159.*

Gordon Giles
Daily Bible readings from Ash Wednesday to Easter Day

FASTING AND FEASTING

An extract from
Fasting and Feasting

We know that food and drink are fundamental to life, yet how many of us have ever thought about what the Bible has to say on the subject? BRF's Lent book for 2009, by *New Daylight* contributor Gordon Giles, takes food as its focus. The Lenten fast concludes with the Easter feast, and, in between, *Fasting and Feasting* examines a range of issues from hospitality to our stewardship of the world's resources. This abridged extract is taken from the first two readings in the book.

Shrove Tuesday

We cannot overemphasize the influence of Jewish tradition on the Christian faith, and nowhere is it more prevalent than in the various rituals and attitudes we have with regard to our food. The central rite of the Christian faith, the Eucharist, owes a tremendous amount to the Passover feast, from which it evolved. Our approach to feasting is hardly a Christian invention and the flipside, the fast, also has origins in Jewish practice. As we embark on a food tourist's journey through Lent, we will surely find ourselves spending time at the tables of both Passover and Holy Communion. We will also find ourselves examining tables today and questioning our relationship with food in this day and age. While climate change often steals the headlines, recent government health warnings

against obesity suggest that it is as great a problem, yet at the same time many people strive to obtain the slim figure of a supermodel and eat very little. In obscene contrast, the populations of some nations starve. It is no longer obvious that food is always a blessing, and it is timely to consider food as a multidimensional aspect of today's economical, physical and spiritual life.

Before we begin, it is Shrove Tuesday, the spiritual equivalent of the day before the morning after! … Shrove Tuesday is not really a feast day as such. It is rather a day prior to a fast day, which is not quite the same thing. Its very name speaks of repentance rather than indulgence and it is good to remember that, while the aroma of maple syrup and pancakes wafts heavenward. 'Shrove' comes from the old English word 'shrive', which means to impose a penance.

Thus it was the priest's role to 'shrive' a person: to hear their confession, allocate them penance to amend for their sins and to pronounce God's forgiveness. To be 'shriven' is to have made one's confession and been absolved. The Reformation theologians were rightly concerned about the potential abuses of a mechanistic approach to forgiveness, especially where money changed hands, but it is ironic that Shrove Tuesday is now more associated with gluttony than penitence. Originally, the period from the Sunday before Ash Wednesday… through to the Tuesday was known as 'Shrovetide' and Christians were expected to make confession and receive absolution, in preparation for the great fast of Lent that begins tomorrow.

During that fast, comestibles such as meat, sweet things, fatty food, sauces or anything apparently extravagant would be abandoned until the Easter feast. This tradition is still very much alive, manifesting itself when people give up chocolate or alcohol for Lent. Early tradition also gives us the threefold discipline of prayer (justice towards God), fasting (justice towards self), and almsgiving (justice towards others). The use of the Gloria at the Mass, and Alleluias, were dropped in Lent, and a general feel of austerity was cultivated. Another devotional tradition also developed, in which this very book stands. Early Christian converts went through a process of instruction prior to baptism during the Lent season (in fact, that is how we acquired Lent in the first place). This was a discipline not only of self-denial but of learning, and the idea of reading books for Lent has descended from that desire for knowledge and truth, so that when Easter Day comes we are not only purer but more knowledgeable about the faith we profess and celebrate. St Benedict declared in his Rule that reading and study were important for any monk, but especially in Lent, when each day a book should be read 'straight through'.

It is in the spirit of this tradition that I offer you this volume, not so much to be read straight through but to be tasted daily, rather like a journey around the table of the Bible, or like a 46-course banquet. Each day's 'plate' will complement the others while, I hope, being tasty on its own… In Lent it is good to taste and see the goodness of the Lord, perhaps in a different way, bringing out different or new flavours. This year, try a biblical diet of feasting as well as fasting, in which we shall consider passages that are either obviously or subtly about food or drink, or about the Eucharist, or that point us forward to the heavenly banquet to which our Lord Jesus Christ invites each and every one of us.

So as we fast and feast together this Lent, it remains only for me to wish you *bon appetit*!

Ash Wednesday

Yet even now, says the Lord, return to me with all your heart, with fasting, with weeping, and with mourning; rend your hearts and not your clothing. Return to the Lord, your God, for he is gracious and merciful, slow to anger, and abounding in steadfast love, and relents from punishing. Who knows whether he will not turn and relent, and leave a blessing behind him, a grain-offering and a drink-offering for the Lord, your God? Blow the trumpet in Zion; sanctify a fast; call a solemn assembly; gather the people. Sanctify the congregation; assemble the aged; gather the children, even infants at the breast. Let the bridegroom leave his room, and the bride her canopy. Between the vestibule and the altar let the priests, the ministers of the Lord, weep. Let them say, 'Spare your people, O Lord, and do not make your heritage a mockery, a byword among the nations.'

JOEL 2:12–17

We saw yesterday how the traditions of Shrovetide have their origins in medieval confession and absolution; there are also similarities to Jewish Passover ritual. As we begin Lent, this passage from Joel is read in many churches today. In his brief work of prophecy, Joel declares the 'day of the Lord', the day on which God appears in a blaze of glory but also heralds drought, famine and anguish (see 1:15–18; 2:1–2). He calls for a widespread and complete manifestation of repentence: fasting, weeping and mourning. The tradition of tearing clothes as a sign of grief is not enough: it is time to tear our hearts and return to the Lord. Everyone—men, women, the old and the young—is to participate in a communal ritual of fasting and prayer that acknowledges guilt and indicates to God their sincerity and love.

If the people did what Joel proposed, it must have been quite a sight. Just imagine the whole of our nation or community united in penitence or sorrow for sin. That would be a real start to Lent, wouldn't it? And it would mark a great contrast with our normal practice: it is hard to get people to come to church on Ash Wednesday, the news media do not mention the significance of the day, and there seems to be just as much sin, pain and grief around as there is on any other day. If people do know about Lent, they do not understand it in the way that Joel understands a general fast. For many, Lent is about 'giving something up', and in this spirit we have created traditions that relate to the spiritual fast of Lent in a physical way. Where there are food traditions for eating up surplus supplies on Shrove Tuesday, there is an inevitable dimension in which we think of future deprivation as inspiring and condoning a little gluttony. It works on a simple level: eat something nice, then deny it to yourself and return to it at the end of the fast, when you will appreciate it all the more. In this way, the spiritual season is physically marked out, but it is very different from what Joel had in mind.

The danger is that the physical dimensions, which are supposed to indicate or underline a spiritual attitude, actually replace it. Lent is not really about 'giving something up'. Giving something up is about Lent. Lent is a period in which we are invited to renew our relationship with God, to 'deny ourselves' and 'take up the cross'. If there is something that comes between us and God, it is good to abandon it in Lent, not only in order to draw closer to God but also to engage in the spiritual discipline of self-denial. There is no point in giving up chocolate, alcohol, sugar, caffeine or some activity if doing so is actually quite easy. Lent is not about what you give up, but about what you do. Sadly, though, over the years, Lent has been perceived negatively as a period for saying 'no', when it is far more challenging and edifying to see it as a period in which we say 'yes' to God as well as 'sorry'. Admittedly, that may involve saying 'no' to ourselves at times.

Fasting is not simply about not eating or giving up certain foods. It is about being humble in the presence of God (Isaiah 58:3–4; Ezra 8:21). The first reference to fasting in the Bible comes when David fasts after his indiscretion with Bathsheba has led to her pregnancy, and he prays that the child may be spared (2 Samuel 12:16). Fasts soon became public events and days of fasting were declared, usually by the elders of the community... Fixed fasts were not very common, except that of the Day of Atonement (Yom Kippur), instituted in Leviticus 16:29, which was the fast that hindered Paul's journey to Rome (Acts 27:9). Later, fixed fasts were declared, as in Zechariah 8:19, after the temple was destroyed.

There are two fixed fasts in the Christian calendar. One is today and the other is Good Friday. Flanking Lent for hundreds of years, they are just as useful and relevant today as they ever have been. Many today will receive the imposition of ashes on their foreheads as a mark of penitence—an outward sign of the inward grace of forgiveness granted by God, through the saving work of Christ on the cross, to his faithful people in this faithless and sinful age. Thus it is today that we begin Lent, with humility in our hearts, prayers on our lips and ashes on our heads.

Lord Christ, may we remember that we are dust, and to dust we shall return. Help us turn away from sin to be faithful to you. Amen

To order a copy of this book, please turn to the order form on page 159.

Exploring Holy Communion creatively

Margaret Withers

Imagine a family gathered around the table for supper. It is a special meal: candles are lit, food is enjoyed, wine is drunk and news is shared. Suddenly the youngest child turns to his father. 'Why is tonight different from other nights?' he asks. And, as the full moon shines through the window, his father tells the story of how God delivered their ancestors from slavery and led them over the Red Sea to the promised land.

Every Sunday we call to mind a similar story—how Christ saved us from the slavery of sin through his death and resurrection. We recall it during a meal, the meal he gave us on the night he was betrayed, when he promised to be present whenever we break bread and remember him. One story flows from the other—but, for me, there is one flaw. The Jews place a child in the centre. The party is not complete without him and the story is told in response to his eager questions. How tragic that the Western reformed tradition removed children from the Lord's table and told them the story without the wonder and joy of meeting Jesus through his word and sacrament.

When I was a children's adviser, people would ask me, 'Can we bring the children to the Holy Communion service? How can we involve them?' The early 1990s

were the heyday of all-age worship. The family service was becoming popular with churches, encouraging congregational participation.

At the same time, another group (of which I was part) was finding ways of making the Eucharist truly inclusive. We took the words of the service and the Bible readings and used sign and symbol, music and drama, colour, light and movement to help people, whatever their age or stage of faith, to worship God with their whole selves. Yet inclusiveness stopped at the altar. Children were not allowed to receive Holy Communion.

But we have moved on! Today, children may be admitted to Holy Communion before confirmation in the Church of England. It is policy in the Methodist Church and common practice in the URC. Stress on the importance of the manner of celebrating the service has encouraged worship that is creative and accessible to all while retaining its sense of the presence of God and beauty of holiness.

In my preparation course, *Welcome to the Lord's Table*, I wrote that if children were present at the Eucharist as communicants, it would change the whole nature of the service. They would be present as of right, rather than being 'allowed' to come in. It was important to review the service and see how it could relate to everyone: if it was not good enough for children, it was probably not good enough for adults, either. If children were admitted to Holy Communion, it was as part of a continuous process that led up to confirmation and beyond. Parents and church leaders needed to help them to grow in their faith and understanding of the significance of Holy Communion as part of their nurture.

It was from this that the idea came for the book *Creative Communion*. Youngsters who had been admitted to Holy Communion at an early age needed to grow in their discernment of the sacrament and how to live it out in their daily lives. My co-author, Tim Sledge, is one of the most creative priests I know, with wonderful flair and imagination. He suggested that, as the Lord made himself known in a meal among friends, we should base the book on the theme of meals and eating together.

Creative Communion is designed in the shape of a letter 'Y'! The stem explores the Eucharist as a four-course meal, with the basic ingredients enhanced by music, drama, colour and movement. It discusses the place of children as part of the worshipping family and as communicants, and the evangelistic angle of the service. The Jews keep an empty place to welcome the stranger to the Passover table. How do Christians welcome the visitors, the enquirers or those on the fringe of society to our meal?

The branches of the 'Y' are two sets of six workshops. Each session explores a part of the service creatively. The all-age programme includes teaching and practical activities, with time for reflection and planning how to incorporate some of the ideas into the Sunday service. The course for youngsters, 'Food, glorious food', focuses on meals, including cooking, eating and discussion on how to live out the eucharistic life in our daily lives at home and in school.

'Can we bring the children to the Holy Communion service? How can we involve them?' These questions are still being asked, but they are easier to answer today. Children can and should be present at the service. Celebrating it creatively does much to give every person an experience of the presence of God, and the youngest may share fully in the Lord's own meal.

To order a copy of Creative Communion, *please turn to page 159.*

Barnabas RE Days

Jane Butcher

'Privilege', 'inspiring', 'challenging', 'fun' and 'tiring' are all words that might be used to describe the experience of a *Barnabas* RE Day. Having only joined the *Barnabas* team in September 2007, these days are still quite new to me and I am only just getting to the point of having led each of the packages available at least once.

One of the notable aspects of leading these days across the country is that we rarely get two identical or even very similar experiences, as the children's responses vary considerably. This keeps us, the *Barnabas* team, on our toes and also allows us the opportunity to learn from the children and adapt what we do as a result.

Often we get the chance to start the day in school by leading collective worship—possibly more well-known as 'assembly'. This gives the school the chance to meet us, to discover what the day might be about, and to begin to experience the creative ways used to explore a theme. Throughout the day, we will usually work with various class sizes, covering children aged from 4 to 11 years.

Children are often very good at expressing their thoughts and feelings and it is a privilege when they share those responses with us during the day. It is encouraging when a child comes to us at the end of a session with words such as 'fab, brill, ace, cool, wicked'—all of which mean that they have enjoyed their time! For me personally, though, it is when a child shares their insight into faith, or says something about the faith journey that they are on, that we receive the greatest sense of encouragement and inspiration for what we do in *Barnabas*.

You may be asking, 'How can I help with this ministry?' I know that many of you pray for the *Barnabas* team, and we very much appreciate your prayers. RE Days are great but they can be very tiring. The journey to and from a school is sometimes smooth and pleasurable but, at times, it can be long and frustrating, with much of the journey taking place in the early hours. We value your prayers for safety as we travel, and for the energy and creativity needed to offer the very best that we can to the staff and children with whom we are working in school.

Please do also pray for the people in the *Barnabas* RE Day freelance team who take on bookings if Lucy, Martyn, Chris or Jane cannot do a requested date. The people within this team are based around the country and, between them, have many gifts including music, drama, dance and mime. We are very grateful to them for their input and for their willingness to be a part of this work. The team is growing in number, and we would appreciate your prayers that the Lord would guide us as we decide when it might be appropriate to expand the team further in specific areas of the country.

Maybe you feel you are not able to be involved in a practical way with your local schools, but perhaps you could consider praying for them—the children, staff and governors. Some may have parents' prayer groups that would appreciate your involvement, or it might be possible for you to have a map of the local area at home, using it to pray for children in certain roads or areas at different times.

Maybe you do feel you would like to be practically involved in the school, but are not sure how. Many schools offer a number of opportunities for people to help. There are certain legal require-

We value your prayers for safety as we travel

ments that the school needs to fulfil, in order for you to take part, but schools are usually only too happy to have support and help from others.

Some schools have a system whereby adults go into school to listen to individual children read. Some may have a 'buddy' scheme in which an adult will go in to support a child who has particular needs. Perhaps you could consider helping one lunchtime a week, or when a school is putting on a specific event, such as a school fair. All of these occasions offer opportunities to support and encourage the life of your local school.

Children offer a great deal to us and we can benefit and learn from our relationships with them. That in itself is an encouragement to invest in those relationships, but maybe more significant are the words of Jesus himself in Luke 9:48: Then Jesus said to them, 'Whoever welcomes this little child in my name welcomes me; and whoever welcomes me welcomes the one who sent me. For whoever is least among you all is the greatest' (TNIV).

Jane Butcher is a trained teacher and children's worker. Along with Lucy Moore, Martyn Payne and Chris Hudson, she is a key member of the Barnabas *ministry team.*

Mentoring others

Tony Horsfall

Spiritual mentoring is a contemporary way of describing the ancient Christian practice of spiritual direction. The main aim is to help another person to become aware of and respond to the activity of God in their life. It involves prayerful listening, with a minimum of advice-giving: the mentor is simply helping the mentoree to discern for themselves what God is doing or saying. It is a releasing, empowering ministry.

Most of us are familiar with the image of the Christian life as a journey. Spiritual mentoring is about accompanying people on that journey, helping them to see the way ahead and to avoid any pitfalls or dangers. Throughout my own spiritual journey I have benefited enormously from trusted 'guides' who have come alongside me at crucial moments in my life, often informally, sometimes in a more intentional way. I consider it an enormous privilege now to offer this kind of accompaniment to others, whether in a formal training context, the less formal setting of a retreat, or on a one-to-one basis.

For the last few years I have been leading a mentoring programme in Singapore. This tiny island state has a population of about 4 million and is modern, progressive and sophisticated. Churches are flourishing, but some congregations appear very 'driven'. This, coupled with

the frantic pace of life, has resulted in lots of believers exploring a more contemplative approach, seeking a deeper reflective walk with God.

I developed the mentoring programme to meet this need. There are six modules, taken over a two-year period. Each module centres on a chosen text, with a written assignment based on what has been read, and then a tutorial with myself, followed by a Quiet Day or Retreat on the same theme. Each module is designed to help the participants build their inner life and prepare them to help others to do the same. We cover themes such as intimacy with God, knowing our identity as God's beloved children, how to abide in Christ, and how to become a soul friend. The group dynamic is very much part of the process, as is the opportunity for individual time with me. We have just over 20 in the present group from a wide range of churches, including missionaries, church leaders and active lay people.

We are currently reading *The Return of the Prodigal Son* by Henri Nouwen, the chosen text for the second module about our identity in Christ. I continually find (and know from personal experience) that the real challenge is to get the truth of our belovedness from our heads to our hearts. The combination of reading, reflection, group interaction and devotional retreat seems to be effective in helping this movement to take place.

Celtic Christians used to say that a person without a soul friend or guide was like a body without a head. Many people nowadays are discovering for themselves the advantages of having a mentor. Spiritual mentoring enables us to grow as disciples without having to fit into a prepackaged mould. It respects individuality yet holds us accountable for growth and development. This flexibility of approach is well suited to a postmodern world and has much to offer the Church today.

My work as a retreat leader brings me into contact with many such individuals. I find that once people step aside from their everyday concerns in order to focus on their relationship with God, and have unhurried time to relax and reflect, spiritual formation becomes much more natural and attainable. I continue to be amazed at the importance of 'holy listening' as part of this process. Once individuals feel safe and respected, and know they can open themselves up in the context of loving acceptance, real progress can be made in allowing God to do that deeper work in their lives.

Often I will journey alongside people simply for the time of retreat. We may follow up with an exchange of emails afterwards, but often geography will keep us from developing an ongoing relationship. Occasionally, a more long-term connection is made with someone who lives nearby and we can meet more regularly. This meeting may be to talk about specific issues (groans), to explore the way ahead (guidance) or to help someone draw closer to God (growth).

There is currently a great need to develop spiritual mentors who can help others to grow in Christ—people who have a real experience of God themselves, are good listeners, and have the wisdom that comes from knowing scripture and having lived a bit. They must be humble and self-aware, have a genuine love for others and be able to keep confidences. Above all, they must be dependent upon God, in tune with the Holy Spirit, and of a prayerful disposition.

Tony Horsfall is a freelance training consultant and retreat leader, and is the author of Mentoring for Spiritual Growth *(BRF, 2008). His website can be found at www.charistraining.co.uk. To order a copy of* Mentoring for Spiritual Growth*, see page 159.*

New Daylight © BRF 2009

The Bible Reading Fellowship
15 The Chambers, Vineyard, Abingdon OX14 3FE
Tel: 01865 319700; Fax: 01865 319701
E-mail: enquiries@brf.org.uk; Website: www.brf.org.uk

ISBN 978 1 84101 513 2

Distributed in Australia by:
Willow Connection, PO Box 288, Brookvale, NSW 2100.
Tel: 02 9948 3957; Fax: 02 9948 8153;
E-mail: info@willowconnection.com.au
Available also from all good Christian bookshops in Australia.
For individual and group subscriptions in Australia:
Mrs Rosemary Morrall, PO Box W35, Wanniassa, ACT 2903.

Distributed in New Zealand by:
Scripture Union Wholesale, PO Box 760, Wellington
Tel: 04 385 0421; Fax: 04 384 3990; E-mail: suwholesale@clear.net.nz

Distributed in Canada by:
The Anglican Book Centre, 80 Hayden Street, Toronto, Ontario, M4Y 3G2
Tel: 001 416 924-1332; Fax: 001 416 924-2760;
E-mail: abc@anglicanbookcentre.com; Website: www.anglicanbookcentre.com

Publications distributed to more than 60 countries

Acknowledgments

Printed in Singapore by Craft Print International Ltd

BRF is a Christian charity committed to resourcing the spiritual journey of adults and children alike. For adults, BRF publishes Bible reading notes and books and offers an annual programme of quiet days and retreats. Under its children's imprint *Barnabas*, BRF publishes a wide range of books for those working with children under 11 in school, church and home. BRF's *Barnabas Ministry* team offers INSET sessions for primary teachers, training for children's leaders in church, quiet days, and a range of events to enable children themselves to engage with the Bible and its message.

We need your help if we are to make a real impact on the local church and community. In an increasingly secular world people need even more help with their Bible reading, their prayer and their discipleship. We can do something about this, but our resources are limited. With your help, if we all do a little, together we can make a huge difference.

How can you help?

- You could support BRF's ministry with a donation or standing order (using the response form overleaf).

- You could consider making a bequest to BRF in your will, and so give lasting support to our work. (We have a leaflet available with more information about this, which can be requested using the form over-leaf.)

- And, most important of all, you could support BRF with your prayers.

Whatever you can do or give, we thank you for your support.

BRF – resourcing your spiritual journey

BRF MINISTRY APPEAL RESPONSE FORM

Name _____

Address _____

_____ Postcode _____

Telephone _____ Email _____

(tick as appropriate)

Gift Aid Declaration

❏ I am a UK taxpayer. I want BRF to treat as Gift Aid Donations all donations I make from 6 April 2000 until I notify you otherwise.

Signature _____ Date _____

❏ I would like to support BRF's ministry with a regular donation by standing order (please complete the Banker's Order below).

Standing Order – Banker's Order

To the Manager, Name of Bank/Building Society _____

Address _____

_____ Postcode _____

Sort Code _____ Account Name _____

Account No _____

Please pay Royal Bank of Scotland plc, London Drummonds Branch, 49 Charing Cross, London SW1A 2DX (Sort Code 16-00-38), for the account of BRF A/C No. 00774151

The sum of _____ pounds on ___ /___ /___ (insert date your standing order starts) and thereafter the same amount on the same day of each month until further notice.

Signature _____ Date _____

Single donation

❏ I enclose my cheque/credit card/Switch card details for a donation of £5 £10 £25 £50 £100 £250 (other) £ _____ to support BRF's ministry

Credit/ Switch card no. ❏❏❏❏❏❏❏❏❏❏❏❏❏❏❏❏❏❏❏

Expires ❏❏ ❏❏   Issue no. of Switch card ❏❏❏

Signature _____ Date _____

(Where appropriate, on receipt of your donation, we will send you a Gift Aid form)

❏ Please send me information about making a bequest to BRF in my will.

Please detach and send this completed form to: Richard Fisher, BRF, 15 The Chambers, Vineyard, Abingdon OX14 3FE. BRF is a Registered Charity (No.233280)

Please note our subscription rates 2009–2010. From the May 2009 issue, the new subscription rates will be:

Individual subscriptions covering 3 issues for under 5 copies, payable in advance (including postage and packing):

	UK	SURFACE	AIRMAIL
NEW DAYLIGHT each set of 3 p.a.	£13.80	£15.00	£17.10
NEW DAYLIGHT 3-year sub i.e. 9 issues	£33.00	N/A	N/A
(Not available for Deluxe)			
NEW DAYLIGHT DELUXE each set of 3 p.a.	£17.40	£21.90	£27.00

Group subscriptions covering 3 issues for 5 copies or more, sent to ONE address (post free):

NEW DAYLIGHT	£11.10	each set of 3 p.a.
NEW DAYLIGHT DELUXE	£14.97	each set of 3 p.a.

Please note that the annual billing period for Group Subscriptions runs from 1 May to 30 April.

Copies of the notes may also be obtained from Christian bookshops:

NEW DAYLIGHT	£3.70 each copy
NEW DAYLIGHT DELUXE	£4.99 each copy

SUBSCRIPTIONS

❑ Please send me a Bible reading resources pack to encourage Bible reading in my church

❑ I would like to take out a subscription myself (complete your name and address details only once)

❑ I would like to give a gift subscription (please complete both name and address sections below)

Your name _____

Your address _____

_____Postcode _____

Gift subscription name _____

Gift subscription address _____

_____Postcode _____

Please send *New Daylight* beginning with the May / September 2009 / January 2010 issue: (delete as applicable)

(please tick box)	UK	SURFACE	AIR MAIL
NEW DAYLIGHT	❑ £13.80	❑ £15.00	❑ £17.10
NEW DAYLIGHT 3-year sub	❑ £33.00		
NEW DAYLIGHT DELUXE	❑ £17.40	❑ £21.90	❑ £27.00

I would like to take out an annual subscription to *Quiet Spaces* beginning with the next available issue:

(please tick box)	UK	SURFACE	AIR MAIL
QUIET SPACES	❑ £16.95	❑ £18.45	❑ £20.85

Please complete the payment details below and send your coupon, with appropriate payment, to:
BRF, 15 The Chambers, Vineyard, Abingdon OX14 3FE.

Total enclosed £ _____ (cheques should be made payable to 'BRF')

Payment by cheque ❑ postal order ❑ Visa ❑ Mastercard ❑ Switch ❑

Card number: ▢▢▢▢▢▢▢▢▢▢▢▢▢▢▢▢▢▢▢▢

Expires: ▢▢▢▢ Security code ▢▢▢ Issue no (Switch): ▢▢▢▢

Signature (essential if paying by credit/Switch card) _____

BRF is a Registered Charity

ND0109

BRF PUBLICATIONS ORDER FORM

Please ensure that you complete and send off both sides of this order form.
Please send me the following book(s):

		Quantity	Price	Total
569 9	Fasting and Feasting (G. Giles)	____	£7.99	____
546 0	Creative Ideas for Quiet Corners (L. Chambers)	____	£6.99	____
587 3	Into Your Hands (K. Scully)	____	£6.99	____
575 0	Growing Women Leaders (R. Ward)	____	£8.99	____
533 0	Creative Communion (M. Withers)	____	£7.99	____
562 0	Mentoring for Spiritual Growth (T. Horsfall)	____	£7.99	____
493 1	Collaborative Ministry (D. Robertson)	____	£8.99	____
565 1	Crying for the Light (V. Zundel)	____	£5.99	____
529 3	Pilgrim's Way (D. Winter)	____	£9.99	____
030 4	PBC: 1 & 2 Samuel (H. Mowvley)	____	£7.99	____
028 1	PBC: Nahum to Malachi (G Emmerson)	____	£7.99	____
046 5	PBC: Mark (D. France)	____	£8.99	____
122 6	PBC: 1 Corinthians (J. Murphy-O'Connor)	____	£7.99	____

Total cost of books £ _____
Donation £ _____
Postage and packing £ _____
TOTAL £ _____

POSTAGE AND PACKING CHARGES				
order value	UK	Europe	Surface	Air Mail
£7.00 & under	£1.25	£3.00	£3.50	£5.50
£7.01–£30.00	£2.25	£5.50	£6.50	£10.00
Over £30.00	free	prices on request		

See over for payment details. All prices are correct at time of going to press, are subject to the prevailing rate of VAT and may be subject to change without prior warning.

PAYMENT DETAILS

Please complete the payment details below and send with appropriate payment and completed order form to:

**BRF, 15 The Chambers, Vineyard,
Abingdon OX14 3FE**

Name _____

Address _____

_____

_____ Postcode _____

Telephone _____

Email _____

Total enclosed £ _____(cheques should be made payable to 'BRF')

Payment by cheque ❑ postal order ❑ Visa ❑ Mastercard ❑ Switch ❑

Card number: ⬚⬚⬚⬚⬚⬚⬚⬚⬚⬚⬚⬚⬚⬚⬚⬚⬚⬚⬚⬚

Expires: ⬚⬚⬚⬚ Security code ⬚⬚⬚ Issue no (Switch only): ⬚⬚⬚

Signature (essential if paying by credit/Switch card)_____

❑ Please do not send me further information about BRF publications.

ALTERNATIVE WAYS TO ORDER

Christian bookshops: All good Christian bookshops stock BRF publications. For your nearest stockist, please contact BRF.

Telephone: The BRF office is open between 09.15 and 17.30.
To place your order, phone 01865 319700; fax 01865 319701.

Web: Visit www.brf.org.uk

ND0109